Job Smarts

Skills for Winning in the Work Place

RAY DREYFACK

Ferguson Publishing Company, Chicago, Illinois

Editorial Staff:
Project Editor: Andrew Morkes
Editor: Anne Paterson
Proofreader: Anne Paterson
Indexer: Sandi Schroeder
Cover Design: Sam Concialdi

Library of Congress Cataloging-in-Publication Data

Job smarts: skills for winning in the workplace
          p. cm.
Includes index.
   ISBN 0-89434-345-9 (pbk. : alk. paper)
1. Compensation management. 2. Promotions. 3. Negotiation in
business.
HF5549.5.C67 W49 2001
650.14--dc21

                                        2001000920

Copyright©2002 by Ray Dreyfack

Published and distributed by
Ferguson Publishing Company
200 West Jackson, 7th Floor
Chicago, Illinois 60606
800/306-9941
http://www.fergpubco.com

Printed in the United States of America
Y-9

DEDICATION

For Tess

My loving wife and indispensable right hand.

ABOUT THE AUTHOR

Raymond Dreyfack is a professional business writer with more than 30 years of experience in systems, management, marketing, sales and personnel training for business and industrial firms.

He has contributed numerous articles to leading sales, management, and business publications. A former editor and co-publisher of *Profit Improvement News,* he also held the position of Systems Director with Faberge Perfumes Inc., and was a lecturer at New York University Management

He has published several books on management, sales, marketing, and writing. These include: *Making It In Management the Japanese Way, Profitable Salesmanship in the '80s, Sure Fail — the Art of Mismanagement,* and *Achieving Financial Independence as a Freelance Writer.*

ACKNOWLEDGMENTS

From a human relations and career standpoint, I owe a great deal to more people than space here could accommodate. High on my list are Chief Editor Richard L. Dunn, Senior Editor Cheryl Firestone, and the wonderful staff at *Plant Engineering* Magazine; my number one management guru, educator, and consultant Leonard J. Smith; Senior Editor Howard Cady of William Morrow & Company; Senior Editor Robert Preyer of Doubleday; Senior Editor Tom Power of Prentice-Hall; Bert Holtje, my favorite agent; William Harrison Fetridge, (deceased) chairman and founder, The Dartnell Corporation; Wilbur Cross, writer and entrepreneur; Robert E. Levinson, Marketing Vice President, Lynn University; and, of course, my dear friend, Cal Clements (long since deceased) and editor/writer and public relations guru Richard Riley Conarroe, both of whom taught me how to put words together into sensible and logical sequence.

TABLE OF CONTENTS

INTRODUCTION

WHAT'S IN IT FOR ME?

A TALE OF TWO GRADUATES

Jim Evans and Dale Brown were pals since their early days in college. Engineering majors, they graduated in the top third of their class with bachelor of science degrees. Jobs were as plentiful then as they are today. The two friends applied for work in an auto parts manufacturing plant. Both were hired at a salary of $30,000.

A year later Jim's boss has only good things to say about him. His salary, after two raises, is now $33,000. He has been promoted to group leader and has advancement to supervisor in his sights. Jim enjoys his job, gets along well with his boss, and crows about his employer. He has a bright future and knows it.

Dale, unfortunately, is in a boat that has leaked from the outset. He thinks of quitting and finding himself a "good job." His wage increase during the year was only a token amount. Unlike Jim, Dale is spinning his wheels. He is disappointed and frustrated and blames the "bad breaks" he's been getting. The "circumstances" are at fault, not Dale.

WHY?

The Question Is Clear: Here we have two friends who set off from the same starting line, same employer, same background, same education, same mental capability; why does one wind up successful, the other floundering? Why should Jim's outlook be bright, while Dale sees only bleak prospects ahead? If this book does its job, it will answer these questions. Not in terms of Jim or

Dale, of course, but in terms that you can apply to your unique individual standpoint. If this book—*in cooperation with you*—does its job, it will help ensure that you wind up not like Dale, but like Jim.

It has been estimated that this year more than two million college grads will enter the competitive, unforgiving marketplace. Countless others will crowd in from high schools and community colleges. If experience holds true, an untold number of jobholders will wind up dissatisfied, disappointed, bored, unfulfilled, in conflict with their bosses or coworkers, subjected to unacceptable pressures and stress. We don't know why Dale is floundering in his career. This book is about you, not Dale. But if you are a student nearing graduation, about to start your first job, or one of the vast army of grunts already in the marketplace who are frustrated and dissatisfied with their jobs, you can be sure of one thing. As studies repeatedly show, one or more of the 10 conditions (listed above) will be the career roadblocks you will need to overcome to achieve the income and status you deserve.

THE 10 PERILOUS PITFALLS

1. You have attitude problems.
2. You are lost in the shuffle.
3. You are being outsmarted.
4. You are out of the knowledge loop.
5. You are too laid back and timid.
6. You don't know the right people.
7. Your boss is working against you.
8. You picked the wrong employer.
9. You are not bottom-line oriented.
10. You are fearful of change.

WHO, ME?

Yeah, you! Your initial impulse may be, "No way, not me!" But if your situation is even close to typical, case history after case history in this book will convince you otherwise.

We are going through a period of unprecedented economic uncertainty. Companies are being reorganized, restructured, reengineered, reinvented. Contradictions abound. Despite skilled worker shortages, departments and divisions are being delayered, multitudes of employees downsized. Change, once the exception, is now the norm. Flextime, not so long ago rare, is today fairly common. Employee mobility has rocketed. Employers are more often wooing applicants than the other way around. For many job hunters, newspaper want ads have become obsolete. As Tevia told his wife in *Fiddler on the Roof,* "It's a new world, Goldie!"

> "How you respond to the New Economy will impact your career in the near and long term."

Where do you stand in this hodge-podge? How you respond to the New Economy will impact your career in the near and long term. One thing you can count on. Solid career planning was never more critical. But the changing marketplace has rendered old ways of career planning obsolete. Step one in the new planning process is to clearly define who you are and what you want to achieve. Consider your financial and family needs. Pinpoint your personal interests and geographical preferences. Decide what you most like to do and what you do best; almost invariably these two go together. A good fit is essential to success in any career. Define your goals and needs accurately to yourself, and you will be able to make sense to a prospective employer.

For young people starting out, the job market can be a bewildering place. Problems and the endless questions that go with them will proliferate: How to resolve conflict with your boss or coworkers? What to expect in terms of work assignments and compensation? How much money to shoot for, and how to go about getting it? How to beat on-the-job competitors to the punch? How to get in good with your boss? How to win recognition from your boss's boss?

> "Education, when linked to experience, is what transforms entry-level employees into high-level employees."

Don't sell reality short. For each question you pose, add a dozen mistakes you are likely to make. One guarantee we can give you: Regardless of whether you have a high school diploma, college degree, or advanced degree, once you are launched in the New Economy, your education is about to begin.

Robert E. Levinson, vice president of marketing at Lynn University, says, "In the New Economy you are never done learning, sometimes formal, sometimes informal, on the job and off. Education is redeemable in cash, status, self-esteem. Education, when linked to experience," he adds, "is what transforms entry-level employees into high-level employees."

"UNDERPAID" DOESN'T ALWAYS MEAN MONEY

Bob Levinson chuckles, recalling Ellen, a young college graduate with a marketing major, who came to him three years ago for advice. She had two job offers to consider: One from a medium-to-large size company offered her $26,000. The other from a smaller company came in at $24,500.

"So what's the problem?" Bob asked.

Ellen frowned. "I have the feeling that if I take the higher paying job I'll be lost in the shuffle, a tiny fish in a big pond. I could be performing boring repetitive tasks day in and day out."

"And the other job?"

"Oh, I was told I would be assigned diversified work. I'd be switched from department to department, get to know the business from the ground up. I would also get the chance to work directly with department heads and other managers. In fact, the supervisor I would report to assured me I would never be bored, that working for him would be a learning experience."

Bob nodded. "There are no guarantees," he said. "But if I were in your shoes I think I would opt for the lower paying job. Your actual pay could be much higher."

The young lady's face brightened. "That's the feeling I had, but I didn't want to feel like a dummy taking the low paying job."

"Not at all. You'll make up more than the difference in experience."

Several months later Ellen came back to thank the savvy executive for his advice. As an assistant sales director, with bonus and add-ons, she now earns $45,000 a year and is headed no place but up.

EXPERIENCE IS WORTH ITS WEIGHT IN MORE THAN GOLD!

Shortening the time you spend to accumulate experience is a primary purpose of this book.

There are two ways to acquire experience that you will be able to apply to your job:

◆ **Doing the job or task yourself.**
◆ **Learning from the experience of others.**

Step by step, the pages of this book will put you on stage with employees in diverse fields and industries who were tripped up by the 10 Perilous Pitfalls pinpointed on page two. Also recounted will be stories of savvy career planners who successfully overcame or avoided those pitfalls—along with a detailed rundown of how they did it and how you can apply their precious experience in your own career. It is no secret to anyone that it takes a great deal of time to acquire sufficient experience to change one's situation from managed to manager, from status quo to status go. It takes guidance as well. With *Job Smarts: Skills for Winning in the Work Place* at your elbow you will chop months —even years—off that time.

Ray Dreyfack
Coconut Creek, Florida

CHAPTER 1:
IMPROVE YOUR ATTITUDE

Problem: Your Attitude is Self-Defeating
RX: Become a Dedicated "Company Man" (or Woman)

> **"Our attitudes control our lives. Attitudes are a
> secret power working 24 hours a day, for good or bad."**
> —Charles Simmons, Author and Theologian

When the president entered the sales department he strolled up to Jim and Mary, young trainees just out of college. He smiled brightly, shook their hands, and chatted with them. Trainee number three, Sally, didn't seem to exist. She could have been a statue. Why did Jim and Mary win recognition and not Sally? Equally important, when salary review time rolled around, why did Jim and Mary receive wage increases and not Sally?

The answer is simple. Jim was an enthusiastic "company man." He made it clear from the outset that the company's business was *his* business. Same thing for Mary. Her "I can do it" image was well known. As for Sally, her ho-hum attitude made her hardly worth noticing.

Famed psychologist William James defines attitude as more important than aptitude. The marketplace confirms his definition.

STATUS QUO OR STATUS GO

Two managers were enjoying a coffee break in the company cafeteria. One said, "If I were a betting man, I'd lay you two to one odds that Ellen will be off the clock and a member of the supervisory staff within 18 months." His friend replied, "If I were a betting man I wouldn't take you up on the wager."

The recent college grad referred to had been hired three months before. No one in the advertising firm Ellen worked for or with would have taken that bet despite the odds. It was clear to all she was headed no place but up. For that Ellen had not only herself to thank but her fiance's dad who was a high level personnel executive for a nationally known food products distributor. Before applying for a job, she went to him for advice. Her question was a simple one. "I don't want to hang around for years in a low-level job. Are there any tips you can give me?"

Her future father-in-law smiled. "One. It's a choice every one of us can make—between status quo and status go."

Ellen nodded. "Spinning your wheels, or moving ahead."

"Exactly. In my experience, nine of 10 employees do no more than what they are told to do if they can help it. Their philosophy coincides with the outmoded Army axiom: 'Never volunteer.' If you opt for status the trick is to get the message across to the powers that be that you are ready and able to pitch in and help out every chance that you get. Volunteer as often as possible. In fact, seek out opportunities to do so. Make a determined effort to bridge what I refer to as the 'Attitude Gap' and sacrifice, if need be, to help achieve department and company goals."

"That makes sense," Ellen replied thoughtfully, and this became her on-the-job attitude.

Ellen's boss, and her boss's boss, were quick to get the message. Ellen rarely turned down the chance to work overtime. If a customer needed information in a hurry she went out of her way to get it, even if it meant working through her lunch hour or break. If someone needed a hand, hers was always outstretched. If a volunteer was needed to work on Saturday, her boss knew he could count on Ellen.

"I make occasional sacrifices," she concedes. "So what's the big deal? It pays off in the end."

How Is Your Attitude Quotient (AQ)?

Are you attitudinally positioned with winning in mind? Can you be counted among the one of 10 employees willing to "bridge the attitude gap," and go beyond the call of duty to help achieve your organization's goals and, at the same time, boost your income and outcome?

Plato wrote, "The life that is unexamined is not worth living." How you feel and think about what goes on in your life shapes both your attitude and philosophy. There's no better time than now to zero in on your personal AQ. As objectively as possible, take the following two-part quiz. Then rate yourself at the end of each part.

(Note: If you do not own this copy of Job Smarts, *then be sure to make a photocopy of this quiz before you mark your answers.)*

Part I—Your Personal Values and Needs	YES	NO
1. Would you say money is *not* the most important thing in life?	—	—
2. Do you have clearly defined personal and family goals?	—	—
3. If asked, would you refuse to do something unethical on the job?	—	—
4. Are you more ambitious than most friends and coworkers?	—	—
5. Do you have a reputation as a good team player?	—	—

	YES	NO
6. Is self-respect extremely important to you?	___	___
7. Is the respect of others equally important?	___	___
8. Would you say you are something of a maverick?	___	___
9. Would you jump at the chance to run your own show?	___	___
10. Would you willingly share credit for good performance on the job?	___	___
11. Do you welcome constructive criticism?	___	___
12. Do you tend to challenge longstanding procedures and policies?	___	___
13. Do you contribute to social well being in your community?	___	___
14. Would you blow the whistle on a dishonest corporate enterprise?	___	___
15. Are strong family values of great importance to you?	___	___

Rate Yourself

Part I. Score 10 points for each "yes" answer to the questions above. Now add your points and enter the total above. A perfect score of 150 in Part I of this self-assessment test qualifies you as a prime candidate for career growth, assuming you responded objectively. While you deserve credit for leveling with yourself, "no" answers should give you something to think about.

Total _____

<u>PART II—Your Personal Job Skills and Attributes</u>	<u>YES</u>	<u>NO</u>
1. Are you a good communicator?	——	——
2. Do people readily follow your leadership?	——	——
3. Are you a quick study; do you pick up things in a hurry?	——	——
4. Are you a resolute and clear-minded decision maker?	——	——
5. Do people often come to you for help in solving a problem?	——	——
6. Are you good at organizing tasks into proper priority?	——	——
7. Are you unafraid of hard work?	——	——
8. Can you honestly boast computer expertise?	——	——
9. Is your thirst for knowledge unquenchable?	——	——
10. Are you a creative person?	——	——
11. Do you welcome new experiences, respond well to change?	——	——
12. Are you good at selling your ideas?	——	——
13. Are you good at fixing things?	——	——
14. Do you get along well with coworkers; do people like you?	——	——
15. Do you know what kind of work you enjoy most and do best?	——	——

Rate Yourself

Part II. Score 10 points for each "yes" answer to the questions above. Now add your points and enter the total below. If you entered "yes" to all questions in this part of your self-assessment test—congratulations! Now you really have it made; that's assuming you had the guts to be completely objective. If you answered "no" once or twice, don't worry. It will give you something to ponder. Of course, if you're the one in a carload with perfect

Total ————

scores on both Part I and II for a grand total of 300 points, our only comment is this: Your bowling score should be so good.

Now Take It a Dimension Further

Wait a minute! You're not finished. You are not yet fully acquainted with yourself. Most people who work for a living believe—rightly or wrongly—that they are underpaid. If you fill this slot, the question we ask is: How do you define "underpaid"? How much more do you want to make now or in the foreseeable future? Are you shooting for **RICH?** Or would **comfortable** satisfy you? Specifically, how badly do you really want the items listed below? How much sacrifice are you willing to make to get them? Soulsearching and answering the following questions may help.

1. *Do you want to be able to afford a home of your own? A modest abode? Or a luxurious showplace?*
2. *Do you want to live in a posh neighborhood? Or will a simple middle-class neighborhood satisfy you?*
3. *How important in your scheme of things are exotic travel and luxurious vacations?*
4. *What is the ideal climate for you and your family? What would you sacrifice to achieve it?*
5. *Is money of overriding importance in the job you are shooting for? Would you settle for less with other values in mind (coworkers, convenience to workplace, status, "work itself" satisfaction, etc.)?*
6. *What about recreational activities? Entertainment? Sports? Are you an active fun-loving person? How much are you willing to sacrifice in fun time to add important money to the kitty? Or, put another way: What's more important to you—high level executive status and luxurious living, or having spare time to indulge your pleasures?*

7. *Is it important to you to be an active member of your community?*

8. *How much does it mean to you to be close to your family and longtime friends?*

9. *What about access to education and cultural opportunities (music, theatre, museums, etc.)? How does that rate in your career planning in contrast to money?*

10. *What about the people you love? Your family? Your significant other or spouse? How important is what they want in your career planning scenario?*

It's not easy to quantify the items above. But in shaping your job and life goals these questions should give you something to think about.

ARE THE CARDS REALLY STACKED AGAINST YOU?

You are at a dead end, frustrated. Not appreciated. Nothing seems to work. Does this ring a bell as it applies to you? If so, welcome to the club. In the marketplace these days gripes roll out faster than a spilled bag of marbles.

- *"I've been bypassed for promotion. What's wrong with me?"*
- *"I'm overdue for a raise. My boss is ripping me off."*
- *"I don't get the credit I deserve."*
- *"My boss is playing favorites, and I'm not one of them."*
- *"There's no chance for advancement. I'm going to switch jobs again."*
- *"There's no point in working hard. You don't get recognition for it."*
- *"I get a rotten deal around here because I'm black." (Or Hispanic, or a white male, or too young, or too old, or a woman, or Jewish, etc.)*

Articulated or not, such thoughts are in the hearts and minds of untold numbers of people. Millions of wage earners at all levels—managers, supervisors, salespeople, entry workers, line and staff personnel—are underpaid and under-appreciated, or they believe they are. But as evidence proves more often than not, employee abuse occurs not at the hands of the employer but is self-inflicted by the griper. Victims blame circumstances and a hodgepodge of situations and events that may or may not be related.

A fact of life in this changing marketplace is that whether we get ahead or are left behind is not the function of our environment but of our actions and responses to the challenges we face. In a nutshell—our attitude.

■ Me-Oriented Charley B.

Attitudinal self-abuse usually starts from day one. In fact, it often prevents day one from starting at all. Take the example of me-oriented Charley B.

Charley, having received his high school diploma, knew all about the shortage of smart and talented workers in almost any industry you could name. With this thought in mind he figured, why undergo the time and expense of a college education? Charley owned a computer and was an experienced user of email. He had a good personality and would make a crackerjack salesman. Instead of shelling out money on more educational grind, it was time to start shoveling it in. With on-the-job training he would be banking big bucks in no time at all. With this idea in mind, Charley started checking the want ads and started to interview.

But instead of being grabbed up by a hungry employer, the response was repeatedly thanks but no thanks. The following typical interview at a sporting goods distributor may give you some idea why.

Employer: Well, Charley, you did well in school. You have a good appearance and a nice personality. Our sales training program runs eight weeks, after which you will be sent into the field as a trainee for three more months with an experienced rep. Do you think this program might interest you?
Charley: It sure would!
Employer: Why do you think you would do well selling for this firm?
Charley: Well, as you say, I have a good personality. People like me.
Employer: Specifically, what do you think you can contribute to this company's profit performance? Do you have any ideas about how you would cover your territory?
Charley: Uh, not exactly. I guess that would come later.
Employer: I see. Do you have any questions?
Charley: Yes I do. How much vacation would I receive? What's your policy on sick leave and insurance benefits? How many paid holidays would I get? How often would I receive wage increases? Would I get a discount on sports equipment?
Employer: We'll discuss all of that if we decide to hire you. You will be notified in the mail.

Get the message? Charley apparently didn't. The reply he got in the mail began with, "We regret to inform you...." A response Charley kept getting again and again. Can you figure out why?

The answer is simple. The employer—every employer—has one primary interest above all others. Profit performance. The bottom line. Charley's primary interest was Charley. The interviewer wanted to hear from Charley what he could do for the company. Charley wanted to know what the company could do for him. He was attitudinally focused on himself. So long as he maintains this focus exclusively he will always wind up a loser.

Charley B., not surprisingly, is a charter member of a heavily populated club of gripers who feel the cards are stacked against them. But we'll leave it to you to decide: In Charley's case, who is stacking the cards? The marketplace—or Charley himself.

HIT-OR-MISS DOESN'T WORK

Thousands of anxious moms and dads keep asking thousands of anxious college juniors and seniors: "What do you plan to do when you graduate?"

One common and popular answer is: "I'd like to take a year off and travel."

We won't argue with that. If you can afford it, or if mom and dad are willing to foot the bill, why not?

Many others opt to join the Peace Corps for a year or so. We won't argue with that either.

But face it. At some point you will have to face the hard reality of the marketplace: You are going to have to get out into the marketplace and all by yourself earn a living. *One way or another!* Here we offer a word of advice: If you leave the *how of it* to chance you're in trouble. As experience proves, the men and women who make it big in the marketplace are the ones who do their career planning like pros. Hit-or-miss winding up happy and rich will be a long shot. We know of no better example than Jim to illustrate this point.

"The men and women who make it big in the marketplace are the ones who do their career planning like pros."

■ Jim

Three years ago, after completing his associate's degree at a community college, Jim decided to find himself a job with a future.

"Doing what?" his friend Alan asked.

Jim shrugged. "I'm not sure, but face it: Everyone says the big bucks today are in electronics."

"That covers a wide field," Alan replied. "Software, hardware, programming, systems, E-commerce. You name it."

"I'll check it out, take the best offer I can get."

Jim had some computer training. What young person today doesn't? Unlike Charley, he was smart enough to know how to make a good impression on an interviewer—focus on his contribution instead of what the company could do for him. He had little trouble landing a job as a programming trainee. Today, three years later, he earns a respectable salary as a systems analyst. There's only one problem. He hates his job. Not so much his company as his work. Jim doesn't like computers; he resents being chained to a desk; he hates the endless detail of programming.

Most important, even though Jim is competent, he is not functioning up to his full potential. *Because computer programming and systems isn't the kind of work he **likes** to do!* That is almost invariably the case. People do best what they like to do most.

So now Jim is thinking of quitting his job and getting into something he enjoys more. Maybe this time he'll career plan his next move instead of striking out blindly.

Smart career planning means evaluating the personal values and needs we discussed earlier, assessing your job skills and attributes, and, most important of all—**DETERMINING WHAT YOU LIKE MOST AND DO BEST**—then targeting that field as your goal.

GO ALONG TO GET ALONG

We'll discuss this later in the book, but for the time being keep one essential fact of business life in mind. Etch it in stone in your memory.

THE FASTEST AND SUREST WAY TO GET RICH IS TO CONTRIBUTE BOTTOM-LINE BOOSTING IDEAS TO YOUR EMPLOYER!

■ Arlene

Arlene was ambitious and smart. She believed with author Napoleon Hill that "ideas are the beginning points of all fortunes." Arlene worked as a group leader in the sales department of a home products company, and her career goal was targeted on full supervisor, eventually manager, and after that vice president. Why not? She had the brains. She had the will. She had the moxie.

And she had an idea she was sold on. Arlene had heard about it from a friend in a competing company. The program, dubbed Competitive Cost Comparison, was held responsible for a 12 percent cost reduction in her friend's company. If it worked there, there was no reason it wouldn't work here. In a nutshell, the idea was to tear down competitive products part by part, work up cost estimates for each part and, where the competitor's cost was lower, analyze why and make adjustments accordingly.

Arlene knew that coming up with an idea is one thing; having it accepted and getting credit for it is quite another. Cashing in on an idea in the marketplace is a two-step procedure. Step one is creating and or adapting the brainstorm. Step two is selling it.

Sometimes selling an idea is even harder than getting it.

Arlene was sure her idea would boost bottom-line profits. So she set out to sell it. She discussed Competitive Cost Comparison with key people in her department who added their input to hers. Then, with her supervisor's help, she wrote up the idea and dropped it in the suggestion box. It went through the corporate mill, was reviewed by the Suggestion Committee, and enthusiastically accepted. The results exceeded expectations. Arlene became an overnight heroine. She received a fat suggestion award. More importantly, Arlene was recently put up for the position of supervisor. She is on her way.

It might be interesting to examine how Arlene was able to get her idea submitted and accepted so easily. Her get-ahead secret is obvious: **You Have To Go Along To Get Along.** Arlene is a team player. Since she is all for the team, the team is for her. Her winning attitude and philosophy is expressed in five simple rules:

◆ Stand behind coworkers, and they will stand behind you.
◆ Never denigrate someone else's idea even if it seems foolish.
◆ When a coworker's idea is accepted, pitch in to make it work.
◆ Encourage coworkers to become involved in your suggestions. That way you will make it *their* ideas too.
◆ Don't hog all the credit. Share it generously.

In a nutshell, help others to achieve their goals, and they will help you to achieve yours.

■ Frank Robinson

Frank, 28, enjoys the distinction of being the only person under the age of 30 in his organization's history to have won a promotion to senior vice president. When he became one of eight senior VPs, a dinner was held to celebrate his appointment by the company's president. Two days later a columnist from the local newspaper showed up at the metal products company to interview Frank for an article he was writing that featured unusual success stories. His opening questions were simple and obvious.

Writer: *"Do you or your wife have family ties to any of the company's top brass or major stockholders?"*

Frank: *"No sir, nothing like that."*

Writer: *"Are you, or is anyone in your family, a major stockholder?"*

Frank: (smiling) *"That's a nice thought, but the answer is no."*

Writer: *"When did you start working here?"*

Frank: *"Four years ago, at age 24, in the advertising department."*

Writer: (shaking his head) *"That's remarkable. How did you make it up the ladder so fast?"*

Frank: *"Not so remarkable when you think of it."*

Writer: *"Explain, please."*

Frank: *"It's really quite simple. We all have our individual wants and needs. The first step, I believe, is to define what yours are, the motivations that determine your personal goals, lifestyle, financial, and everything else."*

Writer: (nodding) *"That makes sense."*

Frank: *"That was my launching pad, you might say. Now, if you work for someone, doesn't it make sense to assume that he or she has wants and needs the same as you. Then, carrying it a step further, doesn't it make sense for you as a subordinate to define those wants and needs and to devote as much of your time and effort to pinpointing those wants and needs and helping as much as you can to fulfill them? Finally, isn't it simple human nature to recognize and reward a person who works hard and makes sacrifices on your behalf? In the workplace, that adds up to wage increases and promotions. My 'secret of success' if you can call it a secret, is simply that. No matter whom I reported to at any given time, I worked harder than anyone else in my group to define my boss's wants and needs and come up with actions and ideas designed to fulfill them. That's all there is to it."*

Writer: *"Doesn't luck enter into it as well? Don't you need to have the right boss, a person who will appreciate and reward your hard work?"*

Frank: *"Absolutely! Luck enters into everything. But here too we have our options. If you feel your boss doesn't give you the credit you deserve, why stick around spinning your wheels? You're free to make a change."*

THE LOWDOWN ON LOYALTY

Loyalty To Your Employer

The new reality of the marketplace puts a new spin on the concept of loyalty to one's employer. The Japanese economy was unique years ago because most large companies ensured workers they would be employed for life. For millions of Japanese, job security was a cherished work value. Words like "downsizing" and "layoff" were unknown. In a book of mine published in that era, *Making It In Management the Japanese Way* (Farnsworth-Dutton), I wrote: "The employee who feels he may be here today and gone tomorrow cannot very well be expected to harbor feelings of goodwill and devoted loyalty to his employer."

1 year	27 percent
2 years	31 percent
3 years	20 percent
4 years	5 percent
5+ years	17 percent

A poll reported in Manpower Inc.'s *Employment Outlook Survey* counsels employers not to "expect relief from the worker shortage of the past two-and-a-half years." It adds, "The pool of skilled and college-educated people remains small, and as unemployment remains low, employers must rely on nontraditional methods of staffing...." Corporations are the wooers, applicants the ones romanced.

Time was not so long ago when job hoppers were looked upon as unreliable by prospective employers. That is no longer the case. In today's economy when many companies with good jobs go begging, jobholders feel they can afford to be independent. Why be loyal, they reason, when you may be out of here within days or weeks? Qualified employees, dissatisfied with their compensation, work assignments, or the way they are treated, know they can give notice today and find a better job tomorrow.

Or can they? We're not so sure.

■ Eddie G.'s Dilemma

Eddie, age 25, a computer wiz in a California software firm, had a great job—$38,000 plus benefits after three years out of college. But the call he got from a headhunter had him hopped up to the hilt. There was an offer of $45,000 from a much larger company—an almost 20 percent wage hike.

The offer was driving him nuts. He couldn't squeeze another nickel out of his present employer; he had already tried. As much as they wanted him to stay, at this point $38,000 was all they could afford. But man, that $7,000 increase was a fat juicy plum. Eddie kept noodling the offer. It was a tough decision to make. His wife Betty refused to make it for him. "I have confidence in your judgment, Eddie." He wished he shared that confidence. He needed help.

Eddie's smart. He asked himself: "Of all the people I know, who is best qualified to give me advice?" The answer came at once. Dr. Lieberman.

Harold Lieberman, Ph.D., had been his guidance counselor when Eddie was a senior. In fact, it was Dr. Lieberman who had initiated the contact that led to his present job. Presented with the facts, what would Dr. Lieberman advise?

His former guidance counselor was delighted to see Eddie as he was to see all returning students. He listened reflectively as Eddie described his dilemma.

"What would I do in your place? I can't answer that. It's your decision to make, a highly personal and individual one. But perhaps I can give you a handle or two to grab onto."

Eddie listened attentively. Dr. Lieberman discussed loyalty to one's employer. "Even that's not clear-cut. We have all kinds of loyalties: to one's self, one's family, one's associates, one's community. On top of that, to deserve loyalty, an employer must *earn it*. Does your employer qualify? That's for you to decide.

"Should you take that 'better offer'? I won't deny that the wage increase is attractive. But money isn't everything; there are other factors involved, a host of questions to answer. Will you fit as well into the new organization as you do at your present employer? The match is of utmost importance. Will you be as excited about the new company's products and services as you are now? Will your opportunity for learning and development be as good? In today's marketplace, Eddie, education is worth double its weight in money. Will you get along as well with your boss and your colleagues? Can you expect your present company to continue growing, giving you the chance to grow with it? Often you can grow faster at a small company than at a giant one. Employees who stuck with Microsoft 20 years ago are multimillionaires today. Will the neighborhood be as good for your family? Schools, shopping, culture, and recreation as convenient? The list goes on.

"You want advice, Eddie? I would recommend a strategy that's older than both of us put together. On a blank sheet of paper enter every relevant question that comes to mind. Then evaluate your answers on a pro and con basis. You'll wind up quickly enough weighing the pros and the cons."

There would be no point in stretching this story. Eddie decided to stay put.

■ Loyalty To Coworkers

Following high school, Emily G. got a clerical job while she attended evening classes at a local community college, majoring in accounting. Committing herself to a tough grind like that, she was obviously ambitious. If she did well at her job in General Office, Emily reasoned, she might get herself a transfer to the accounting department. With that goal in mind, working in the billing section, she produced more bills than anyone in the group.

But her troubles began from day one. They were launched by Peggy, a marginal performer, with an almost dictatorial word of advice. "Slow down. Stop working so hard. You'll get no thanks for it, and you're making it bad for everyone else."

Emily didn't reply. She continued her conscientious performance. Peggy didn't give up trying to slow Emily down. Again, she didn't respond. But Emily was upset. On the one hand she wanted to succeed. On the other she didn't want to make things hard for the other billers and antagonize them. She asked herself: To whom did she owe loyalty—her employer or coworkers?

Billing Supervisor Mike Davidson was smart. He had Peggy pegged as a loser and had observed her carping to Emily. He summoned Emily to a conference room where they could talk in private.

"I noticed Peggy giving you the needle," he said, "and you don't have to tell me what she said. Emily, there are all kinds of loyalty, in business as in life. There's loyalty to your employer and loyalty to your coworkers. There is a third loyalty too—to yourself, to your family and conscience and the honest goals that you set. No one asks you to run yourself ragged; all management wants is an honest day's work

> "No one asks you to run yourself ragged; all management wants is an honest day's work for a fair day's pay. Fulfill that responsibility and you will develop and grow."

for a fair day's pay. Fulfill that responsibility and you will develop and grow. Fail to do so and you'll be a loser like Peggy. Do you read me?"

Emily nodded thoughtfully. She got the message.

A MINDSET THAT CAN'T MISS

The more you learn, the more you earn.

You don't need an advanced degree to appreciate this simple reality. Check the bios and background of any millionaire you could name from Bill Gates and Steve Ballmer to the super-wealthy heads of GE, GM, IBM, Chase Manhattan, or any major corporation that comes to mind. It will confirm the can't fail success formula that results in riches and fame:

Become the in-house expert, and take it from there!

CHAPTER LESSONS

✓ Bridge the attitude gap. Don't let a bad attitude defeat your advancement in the workplace. Get excited about your job, and you will get noticed.

✓ Be a volunteer.

✓ Be a company man or woman.

✓ Don't take a job just because it pays well or because it is part of a fast growing field. Smart career planning involves evaluating your personal values, job skills, and deciding what career you would like to do best, then targeting that job field.

✓ Go along to get along. Be a team player. Help others to achieve their goals, and they will help you to achieve yours.

✓ Learn the wants and needs of your boss and fulfill them.

✓ Evaluate your loyalties to determine how they affect your career goals.

CHAPTER 2: GET NOTICED

PROBLEM: You Are Lost In the Shuffle
RX: Stand Out—Get Found

"The deepest principle in human nature is the craving to be appreciated."
—William James, Psychologist

DARE TO BE DIFFERENT

Talk about using your head and imagination to get ahead. I'll never forget my friend Harry's experience. More years ago than I care to recall, Harry, like myself, was a young junior executive, struggling to boost his income and make a name for himself. His problem was a common one. I lacked the experience and insight at the time to pinpoint and analyze it. But how Harry solved this problem with the help of his uncle has been an inspiration to me over the years.

We were neighbors and friends. We shared our small triumphs and commiserated over why we felt they were too few and far between.

One day Harry, looking more glum than usual, confided, "You know, Ray, sometimes I wonder if it's all worth it." He was being melodramatic, of course.

"If what's worth it?" I asked.

"The whole schtick," he said, "the struggle, beating your brains out to get ahead, make more money."

I'd had the same thought myself more than once. I asked, "What in particular is bugging you now?"

Harry said, "My company employs about 12,000 people, a 100 in my department alone. I'm no more noticeable than a shell on the beach."

"I know what you mean," I replied. Then I made a suggestion."Why don't you talk to your Uncle Jack about it?" Harry's Uncle Jack was a high paid executive in a manufacturing company, earning well into six figures.

Harry frowned. "I don't like crying to relatives."

"Don't cry, interrogate. How can it hurt?"

Harry was frustrated enough to swallow his pride. What his uncle told him changed his life—and mine.

"Harry, *you have to dare to be different.* You have to do something that makes you stand out from the crowd, something that will get you noticed by the people who count," Uncle Jack said.

"Like what?" Harry asked.

Uncle Jack shrugged. "It doesn't matter, so long as it makes the job easier or faster and helps improve the bottom line. Take a hard look in your own backyard, your own department. No one knows the operation better than the people who work there day after day. Pick out the biggest problem you can find. Explore it from every angle. Then brainstorm, come up with something new and different that will minimize or help solve the problem. Original or borrowed, it makes no difference."

This set Harry to thinking. Next day he confided his uncle's words of wisdom to me.

"The biggest problem in my department is space. We need more people but don't have anywhere to put them. The office is packed like a singles bar offering beer on the house. There's no room to breathe."

"So what's your solution?"

"Simple. It works elsewhere; it can work for us. You install a Working Mother's Second Shift."

"Come again?" I said.

"A Working Mother's Second Shift. I read an article about a company where the work kept piling up, just like in our office. They needed more people, but there was no place to put them. So they advertised for experienced personnel interested in working from 6:00 to 10:00 PM three or four days a week. Two mail department people were needed to handle the flock of replies they received. Hundreds of moms who had cabin fever grabbed the opportunity to get out of the house and earn extra money in the bargain. That second shift solved the space problem faster and more economically than doubling the size of the office would have done."

"Sounds smart," I replied.

It was smart. Harry wrote up the idea and became an overnight hero. It was a milestone in his long trip to financial independence. That was a long time ago. Today Harry is a senior vice president at one of the nation's leading banks. His lesson in career advancement worked for me, too. From that day on I started to view the job from a new perspective. What could I do to stand out and be noticed? Subsequent experience taught me that opportunities for such exposure are limited only by one's imagination.

DREAM UP WAYS TO STAND OUT AND BE FOUND

You have a choice: Innovate or vegetate. Smart innovation will make anyone stand out from the crowd and get noticed by the people who count. Here from my personal storehouse of brainstorms is a sample of innovative actions that produced career-boosting results. How many can you adapt to your personal use?

■ Ellen—Profit Improvement

Getting some people to turn in a suggestion is harder than pulling an elephant's tooth. Not Ellen in Inventory Control. When a cost-cutting drive was announced, she sprang into action. After some hard creative thinking and research, she worked up a list of 14 stock items that could be purchased for a lower price than what the company had been paying. Result, Ellen received a write-up in the company publication, a fat suggestion award and, weeks later, a merit increase in pay.

■ Ron—Labor Saving

Ron in Assembly is smart enough to understand that the heaviest cost burden in most companies is direct labor. When he saw an ad for an automatic lifting machine that would permit two employees to do a job long done by three workers in the department, he turned it in as a suggestion. This won him not only a suggestion award, but the kind of recognition that leads to career growth as well.

■ Brad—Conflict Resolution

Chuck and Frank were about as compatible as Snoop Doggy Dogg and Pat Boone. The trouble their frequent run-ins caused each other and the department was disruptive. Assistant Office Manager Brad saw this clearly. Why they still worked on the same team was a mystery to him. Brad sounded out Chuck, then Frank, then had a talk with his boss. "Yeah," his boss said recognizing the problem, "but those guys are veteran employees. I can't fire either of them." "No need to," Brad replied. "I checked it out. There's an opening in Statistical; Frank would love to be transferred there." His boss liked the idea. The headache had been bugging him for months. As Brad knows, there's no better way to help yourself than by helping the boss.

■ Anne—Logistics

The copying machine in Accounts Receivable created a continuing bone of contention. Half the time it was free; the other half, employees were lined up to use it. The lineup delayed work and caused complaints. That is, until Anne's brainstorm solved the problem. The copier in Accounting was used only 15 percent of the time. "Why not put the machine just outside of Accounting?" Anne suggested. "That way it would be accessible to both departments." Her boss liked the idea. Anne liked the write-up she got in the company magazine and the highly favorable entry in her personnel file.

■ Andy—Delegation

Andy in Data Processing sympathized with Mr. Griffen. Although his boss was overloaded with work and lugging home a full briefcase most nights, his workload kept expanding like the belly of a person addicted to ice cream sundaes and eclairs. Now, with the new Claims Analysis Report to get out, it was bigger than ever. Andy was smart enough to realize that Mr. Griffen's problem was his opportunity. "I'd be glad to take over the Claims Report," he suggested. His boss frowned. "It's rather complicated. Can you handle it?" "I think so," Andy replied. "I'd like to give it a try." His boss smiled. "Okay, let's do it."

Get the drift? This isn't the Army, Mr. Jones. Don't be afraid to volunteer. Innovate. Step in and take over. Shake off your natural reticence. It's the way to stand out and get noticed. Whether

STAND OUT AND BE FOUND

What follows is a list of suggested actions you might take to spark the attention of the people who count most in your company:

- Pinpoint a problem and recruit whatever assistance you can to help solve it.

- Zero in on a difficult task shunned by most of your coworkers and volunteer to tackle it.

- Brainstorm about a tough cumbersome job that usually causes friction or delay and figure out a way to make it simpler and more effective.

- If you can, take steps to reduce antagonism and friction between two employees or departments.

- Dream up an effective way to improve customer service.

- Recommend a well-qualified neighbor or friend for employment with your organization.

- Suggest a better, cheaper, or more effective material or tool to do a job.

- Come up with a clever way to save space.

- Suggest a time-saving idea.

- Find a way to reduce waste.

- Dream up an idea to eliminate paperwork.

- Suggest a way to improve office or plant safety and security.

- Find a way to lengthen the life of a piece of equipment or tool.

- Become conspicuously engaged in a volunteer effort in your community.

- Dream up a way to improve your organization's public image.

Each of the above items is a Stand Out and Be Found launching pad in its own right. How many ideas can you add to this list? How many can you put into effect? Consult this list periodically. Keep a record of your progress.

you're fresh out of high school or college or a longtime employee, it never fails to work.

DON'T BE AFRAID TO STIR UP THE POT

Several years ago I landed a job as IBM Manager for a wholesale liquor distributor. I was still a kid. My prior experience included training in IBM equipment in the Army and, when discharged, an IBM operator's job with a liquor wholesaler that led to my current employment. My task was to design and install a system similar to the one I had just left.

The challenge wasn't all that difficult, or so I thought. I knew what had to be done and what equipment and personnel would be needed to do it. What's more, IBM—the blue chip giant— had already sold the installation, designed the system, and specified the required machines. Scheduled delivery was eight months away, which I believed was ample time, for the planning and setup work that had to be done.

It was a great opportunity. A jump from line employee to manager. I felt cocky and proud. Maybe too cocky. My boss, the controller, wisely suggested I spend a few weeks familiarizing myself with the liquor company, its product line, and how the company did business. Day by day my confidence grew. With IBM's equipment and system design what could go wrong?

Hoo hah! The roof caved in. Three weeks after my date of hire my boss showed me the contract that had been signed with IBM. I looked over the specs and did a double take. I read and reread them. A queasy feeling grabbed my gut. It's called fear.

In a quaky voice I asked my boss, "Excuse me, sir. Who drew up these specifications?"

He gave me a look I will never forget. "IBM, of course. Why?"

I swallowed. "They're all wrong. Equipment is missing. The accounting machines don't have all the features required. We will need a collator, which isn't included. Three sorters were ordered; all we need are two."

His face turned whiter than bleached cotton. For several moments he didn't speak. He didn't have to. His thoughts were written all over his face. Who was this pip-squeak kid to challenge IBM's specs? His eyes were cold as dry ice. Small wonder. His job, was on the line, just as mine was.

"Dreyfack [he previously had called me "Ray"], are you telling me you can't set up and operate with the equipment specified in this contract?" He made "Dreyfack" sound like a swear word.

I wondered if he could see me trembling. "I wouldn't say that exactly, sir. But with this setup we'd need twice as many people as the plan calls for. The operation can run, but it would cost much more than projected." I tried to explain why, but it was over his head.

"I'll get back to you," he grunted.

I can tell you, with our first child on the way, I didn't spend a restful night.

It wasn't my boss who got back to me. It was IBM. Next morning at 11 two visitors called; one was the IBM sales rep assigned to the account, and the other was his boss, the divisional manager.

"What's this all about?" the division head demanded.

I explained what it was all about. Fortunately, I knew what I was talking about. So did they. As I laid out the facts, the division head glanced about nervously. In a small voice he suggested, "Let's go to lunch."

They took me to a fancy restaurant. The division head threw a questioning look at the salesman. The rep moistened his lips. "Dreyfack's right," he admitted.

My sigh of relief was audible. Then they tossed me the bombshell. The installation sold to my employer had been designed by a sales rep, now in the hospital, who had suffered a nervous breakdown. He had been in the throes of the breakdown while designing the system.

> "In business, situations sometimes occur that force you to choose between stirring up the pot or taking the easy way out. But short-term gains improperly achieved usually result in long-term loss."

Wow! The implications raced through my mind like fire trucks on the way to a four-alarm blaze. The division head looked somber. "Ray, we're between a rock and a hard place," he confided. "If we concede we were wrong and you're right, they'll probably tear up the contract, and toss you out with it."

It made sense.

"But if you assure management the installation *could* work effectively as designed—but more economically, with a few changes there's a good chance they'll go along with"—he coughed into his hand—"a somewhat revised system."

That made sense too. So we compromised. The system was altered to my specifications and reluctantly approved. When it became operational, it exceeded the company's most optimistic expectations, and was written up in an industry publication as a model setup.

Today, when I think back, the question arises: What if I had decided not to challenge IBM's specs, *not to stir up the pot?* Suppose I had gone along with the original specs and kept my mouth shut? The system would have limped along, and my job would have been saved temporarily. So why didn't I do it? Because the system was flawed and I knew it. Being a party to it would have been not only dumb but also unethical.

In business, situations sometimes occur that force you to choose between stirring up the pot or taking the easy way out. But short-term gains improperly achieved usually result in long-term loss. Had I installed the flawed system, at some point it would have backfired because of the excessive cost burden. Months later I would have been out of a job and my reputation damaged. Morality aside, I had no choice but to stir up the pot.

On the job, if you advance beyond stock clerk or porter, sooner or later you will have hard decisions to make. How you make them will affect your future income and outcome. What kind of decisions? Typical situations from my own experience that may call for pot stirring action—some conscience-related, some not—follow:

◆ Something that isn't kosher is going on in your organization. Conscience aside, if you keep your mouth shut you may be sucked into it.

◆ You see no chance to get out of the underpaid rut you are in. Unless you do something dramatic to stir up the pot, the rut you are in is sure to deepen.

◆ You are being taken unfair advantage of in one way or another. Remain a passive victim and you will continue getting the shaft. Pot stirring time once again.

◆ The person beating you out for the job hike you deserve is blatantly misrepresenting himself, and you're simmering along as a passive bystander. Passive, you vegetate. So what choice do you have?

◆ Your boss has proposed a project you know will hurt the company and your own prospects as well. Your options are clear: Remain silent, or stir.

In the situation related above, I never regretted stirring the pot. That restructured IBM system was a giant stepping-stone in my career.

The best advice I can offer is this: When in doubt, follow your heart and your mind. If the decision you make is to stir up the pot, tackle it bravely and honestly.

GET THEM TALKING ABOUT YOU

When people talk about you, you are a force to contend with, good or bad. People who get talked about are rarely lost in the shuffle. They win acclaim or go downhill, depending on what people say about them. Get the right people to say the right things, and there's no way you can lose.

After Allyson got her high school diploma, she took business courses at a vocational school—good thinking if you decide not to attend college. Now she works in the secretarial pool of a local finance company, where she feels she's as smart as her coworker Gloria, if not smarter. Yet when the boss Mr. Ames needed an executive secretary, Gloria was the one chosen.

It made Allyson wonder: Why did Gloria make it while she was left behind? Constructive wondering.

To find the answer, Allyson talked with other secretaries, her parents, and supervisors with whom she was friendly. Some of the feedback she got follows.

> "When in doubt follow your heart and your mind. If the decision you make is to stir up the pot, tackle it bravely and honestly."

Supervisor #1: Gloria's smart enough to know when to speak up and whose attention to attract.

Secretary #2: She may do unusual things, but they seem to pay off.

Allyson's dad: You're probably better qualified than Gloria, but does anyone besides you know it?

Secretary #3: I don't know, Ally. Maybe Gloria has more of what it takes. (Allyson refused to buy this.)

Secretary #4: Gloria always seems to be in the right place at the right time.

Supervisor: Apparently Mr. Ames knows Gloria and has confidence in her. You might ask yourself: Why doesn't he know me equally well?

Allyson's mom: Oh dear, I wouldn't be upset about it.

But Allyson was upset. It kept bugging her. Why Gloria and not her? Reflecting on the comments that were made and on her own observations, she decided to probe further. What she learned was instructive.

- ◆ Gloria was famous for some of the zany suggestions she had turned in. Most were too wild to get accepted; but others had paid off well enough to keep her name in the limelight.

- ◆ Gloria made no effort to conceal her ambition. She was usually the first to volunteer for overtime when the department was in a bind.

- ◆ Whatever the task, lacking experience or not, Gloria always announced confidently, "I can do it!" If she didn't know how at the time, she made it her business to find out.

- ◆ Improbable as it may seem, Gloria was, in addition to being a good secretary, a good mechanic. If someone had car trouble, Gloria was the one he or she called to check it out. In a nutshell, *she dared to be different.* She stood out like a plum on a pear tree.

"It makes sense," Allyson's brother-in-law, an advertising executive, said in response to these observations. "Even if you are smarter than Gloria, and your imagination is as good, she seems to be one up on you because she understands the importance of attracting attention and getting people to talk about her. It's the same principle that makes advertising pay off. The more often your name comes to the attention of the people who count, the more likely it will be to come to mind when there's a decision to be made in your favor."

"On the job, a good time to take the plunge—even if it may seem reckless at times—is when you have nothing to lose."

TAKE EDUCATED GAMBLES

Famed educator James Conant said, "Behold the turtle. He makes progress when he sticks his neck out."

"Why go out on a limb?" author Frank Scully once asked. His answer: "Because that's where the fruit is."

While mindless risk is foolhardy, a smart gamble often yields rich rewards. The question is when to run a risk and when to stay cool and play it safe. On the job, a good time to take the plunge—even if it may seem reckless at times—*is when you have nothing to lose.*

When a Risk Isn't Risky

■ Ira

Ira, one of three department supervisors, had been nursing the decision for months: To quit or stick it out a while longer. His job stunk. He had gone more than two years without a promotion and had gotten only small token raises to show for his hard work. Department head jobs, for which he was more than qualified, opened from time to time, but they always went to someone else. When he complained, Ralph, his boss, usually placated him with compliments and reassurances. "You're one of my favorite people, Ira. Be patient, your day will come."

Ira's patience had long since expired. As a manager, Ralph was in a position to recommend him for promotion. But he kept putting it off. Ira thought he knew why. Ralph blocked his promotion because he was too useful to him where he was. Ira made decisions Ralph should have made. Ira handled too many projects because Ralph relied on his good work the most. When Ralph was in a bind, he turned to Ira for help.

He was being held back because his boss didn't want to lose him! A not uncommon occurrence in business. Ira was in a dead end job. Why hang around?

Still, after five years with the company, he realized his salary, pension vesting, and other benefits were valuable. He would have no trouble finding another job, but his wage and benefits package wouldn't be easy to duplicate.

Ira's choices were clear:

◆ Shop the market for another job.
◆ Give Ralph an ultimatum to get him a promotion or else he would go over his head and speak to higher management.
◆ Hang in there and hope for the best.

Hoping for the best seemed the worst option. Ira decided to talk it over with his wife, Irene.

Smart lady, Irene. "Tell me one thing," she said. "Given the status quo, would you be willing to stay on the job?"

"No way!"

"Then you have nothing to lose by taking action."

Put that way, it made sense. The next day Ira confronted Ralph head on. "Either I get that promotion or I'm out of here."

His boss blanched, feeling or feigning disbelief.

"I've been spinning my wheels long enough. There's no future for me here."

Ralph gave him a hard look. No harder than the one Ira returned. "I don't know if I can swing it," his boss stalled.

Ira shrugged. "If you can't, maybe Mr. Gorman can."

Ralph blew out his cheeks. "I'll talk to him. Give me a day or two."

"No more than that."

Today the plaque on Ira's desk reads "Department Head." His income boost was substantial.

FACE REALITY: FIND A MATCH IF YOU CAN

Are you lost in the shuffle or stuck in a rut? It adds up to the same thing. Undervalued. Underpaid. A condition crying for action. Check the following case examples to see if one or more strike a responsive note in you. If you find a match, consider the recommended response.

■ General Office

It was the third time in the past six months that Frieda had an idea accepted, only to have Mr. Getts her supervisor claim credit for them, with nothing more than a "thank you" for Frieda. As a result, her boss's image shone, while hers remained dull. A couple of times he threw her a paltry raise, penny-ante stuff. When Frieda complained, Getts shrugged: "That's the real world, honey." Barely restraining her anger, she requested a promotion and pay increase. What she got back was a spiel about the table of organization not calling for it.

Rx: Unwritten law or not, Frieda decided to violate it. She went over her boss's head to Mr. Benson. "I'm being treated unfairly," she complained. The executive frowned. "How so?" When she started to explain, he cut her off. "You'll have to take that up with your supervis—" It was Frieda's turn to cut Mr. Benson off. "Please listen to me." He listened as she ran down the list of ideas Getts had palmed off as his own with no credit to her. A week later Frieda received a nice raise. As for Getts, he doesn't work there any more.

■ Data Processing

Fred was the best programmer in the department, but he wasn't part of the "in-group." Result, when the eligibility list for advanced training was posted, Fred's name was conspicuously absent. When he asked why, his boss shrugged. (Have you ever noticed? Bosses who exploit people shrug a lot.) "Maybe next time around." "When will that be?" "Hard to say." Meaning a year from now or never. And undertrained means underpaid.

Rx: Next morning Fred didn't show up for work. He was too busy setting up interviews. Quitting a job isn't easy; risk is involved. But when you're spinning your wheels, what choice do you have?

■ Bank

Wage information is supposed to be confidential. But the word gets around. When Agnes in the back office learned that Milton, with less seniority and experience, earned 15 percent more than she did, she had a mild case of apoplexy. When Milton couldn't handle a problem, he turned to her for advice. If a task was too hard for Milton, it was reassigned to her. When she complained about the disparity in pay, she was given a halfhearted excuse.

Rx: You take your chances in confronting the boss. But you're worse off if you sit still for abuse. A lawyer friend suggested that Agnes ask her boss if he was familiar with the Equal Pay Act. When he hemmed and hawed in response, she said sweetly, "I would hate to sue my own company." Her increase came through in short order.

■ Advertising Firm

No one was more deserving of promotion to account executive than Jayson, and no one was less likely to get it. Jay's competition for the job included the CEO's son-in-law, niece, and nephew. Jay didn't stand a chance.

Rx: Evaluating his situation, Jay made the only move possible. He got on the Internet and started browsing the job sites.

■ Department Store

Myrna was in line for a wage increase and had a chance to get almost double the increase she was entitled to. All she had to do was accede to her supervisor's demand that she spend a night at a motel with him.

Rx: Myrna wasted no time arguing or reasoning. Tight-lipped and livid, she marched into the Personnel Vice President's office. If it meant losing her job, good riddance. When her charge was investigated, Myrna got her raise and her boss got the gate.

■ Insurance Company

Despite his good work record, Albert kept getting bypassed for the raise he deserved. When he asked his boss why, his boss's nervous answer made it clear that the real reason he was bypassed had less to do with his performance than his being African American.

Rx: Albert had two choices: (1) to resign and possibly experience the same bigotry elsewhere or (2) to sue on the grounds of racial discrimination. Unpleasant or not, he decided to file the charge and won the fight with a knockout.

■ Manufacturer

Tony was a hardworking production supervisor, undervalued and going nowhere, 18 months on the job and no raise in pay. When he griped to his boss the production manager, he conceded the truth of Tony's complaint, then pulled out the company's latest Profit & Loss statement. The company had lost money two years running. "You're lucky to still have a job."

Rx: If that was luck, Tony felt, he could use some ill fortune. After checking his employer's financial condition, Tony realized the company was headed downhill with little hope of reversal. Time to search for greener pastures, he wisely decided. In a job with no future, the risk of losing the job isn't a risk.

The point of these stories is simple. If you are underpaid, underappreciated, and otherwise undercompensated for your work, the situation is only hopeless if you view it that way. For virtually every career-busting problem there's a solution you can find if you have the determination and moxie to ferret it out.

ATTRACT TOP-LEVEL ATTENTION

To advance up the career ladder one small step at a time, the person to impress is your immediate supervisor. To advance with giant steps you need to focus on the person in the top executive suite. Jerry was a skilled and imaginative product manager in the marketing department. His bright ideas had won him suggestion awards and good appraisals during his four years on the job. But he felt his growth was too slow. At age 30 Jerry figured if he didn't make his move soon, he might never make it.

He had an idea for a marketing program he was excited about. He had mentioned it more than once to Arthur, his direct supervisor. But Arthur was always too busy or had some other excuse for putting him off. When Jerry decided to try one more time, his boss's response was annoyance. "I said I'll get back to you when I have the chance."

> "If you are underpaid, underappreciated, or otherwise undercompensated for your work, the situation is only hopeless if you view it that way."

That did it. Protocol or not, he went over his boss's head. Confronting the senior vice president for marketing, he tried to present his idea. The executive cut him short. "Young man, channels of communication have been established for a good reason. The person to discuss this with is your supervisor."

"But—"

"—There are no but's'."

Jerry thanked the manager for his time and left—not only the VP's office, but in due time the company as well. He made an appointment with a search consultant and spelled out his frustration.

A week later Jerry got a call. An appointment had been set up for him with the president of one of his company's competitors. There Jerry described his proposed marketing program in detail. The president was sufficiently impressed to offer him a manager's job similar to the one he had been shooting for at his old company and a nice wage boost.

The point of the story is simple, and the formula unbeatable. Does a quantum leap in both income and status intrigue you? Then dream up an appealing bottom-line boosting idea and bring it to the attention of a high level executive. Top managers are rarely too busy to listen to money-making or money-saving ideas. The bottom line is their number one responsibility.

If your idea is really good but the right ear isn't available, don't lose heart. There are more executive ears in the marketplace than you could shake a P&L statement at.

Are you frustrated by slow (or *no*) growth in your company? There are any number of ways to call top-level attention to what an exceptional person you are:

■ Community Service

When a crusade was launched to recruit surrogate "dads and moms" to give "kids at risk" the help and guidance needed to keep them off drugs and off the streets, Gary in Personnel was at the forefront of those who pitched in with their care and time. His efforts were so successful and productive that they were written up in the local newspapers. The day after he appeared on TV, Gary was summoned to the office of the company president who congratulated him personally. Weeks later it was no surprise to anyone when Gary was named to head up the newly formed Community Relations Department.

■ **Supernumerary**

A supernumerary in the workplace is an extra, or unneeded, person. In any enterprise, labor is a key cost of doing business, supernumeraries create a major drain on profits. Phyllis needed her job but considered herself excess baggage in the Accounts Payable Department. She knew that through a simple change in computer programming the work she did could be dispensed with and the job made more efficient. Pulling in a deep breath, she composed a memo spelling out the how-to and gave it to her supervisor. It was a calculated risk. The suggestion could either put her out of a job or spring her out of her rut. Word of the employee who had been gutsy enough to eliminate her own job spread fast and made its way to the president's desk. This smart executive decided it made good sense to make an example of Phyllis in order to encourage others to follow her bottom-line thinking. Now a supervisor, Phyllis is headed no place but up.

■ **Customers**

One question quiz: Who is the person most important to any for-profit organization? The president? Wrong. You guessed it: the *customer.* One sure way to get top-level attention and recognition if you are a sales rep is to make more sales than anyone else on the sales force. But even for a first rate salesperson, success depends on the territory assigned. In most companies high potential territories go to the most successful long term reps. But if, like Shep, you are just out of college, have little experience, and the territory you cover is only so-so, your chances of topping the sales charts are slim. So Shep found another way to command top-level attention. The way he served customers was so extraordinary that the president kept getting rave letters from customers praising his service. In Shep's book, the customer reigns supreme. He repeatedly went out of his way to go beyond the call of duty in responding to customer problems and needs. In the president's book, too, the customer calls the shots. It is thus only natural that Shep is now a divisional manager.

Problems, needs, and opportunities vary from organization to organization and job to job. But one thing remains constant: High-level executives are driven by a need to . . .

◆ **maintain and build profits**
◆ **keep stockholders happy**
◆ **keep customers satisfied**
◆ **keep employees productive**

Find new and imaginative ways to help fulfill top executives' goals and you will be a sure bet to command high-level attention— and the rewards that go with it.

CHAPTER LESSONS

✓ Dare to be different. Stand out from the crowd. Come up with ways to make the job easier, faster, or improve the bottom line.

✓ Get people talking about you. Don't be afraid to make suggestions, no matter how crazy they seem. Be ambitious. Adopt an "I can do it" attitude.

✓ Smart gambles often yield good results. Take the plunge (speak up about an unproductive work situation or even leave a job) when you have nothing to lose.

✓ Developing bottom-line boosting ideas will help you get high-level attention and move up.

CHAPTER 3:
COMPETE LIKE A PRO

Problem: You Are Being Outsmarted
Rx: Learn To Compete Like a Pro

TOUGHEN UP TO COMPETE STRONG

The past decade has witnessed unprecedented structural and attitudinal changes in enterprises major and minor. Corporations are being reinvented, reengineered, and restructured. Employees are being rocked and rolled like a rowboat in a hurricane. International Survey Research reports that "the '90s have seen an overall decline in employee satisfaction levels...employee identification with and commitment to their employers have substantially declined."

Today, more people than ever are cashing in on the opportunities triggered by change. More employees are making the transition from low to high pay. More millionaires are being created. What can we conclude from these events? If you have the imagination and determination to respond aggressively and courageously to the challenges of change in the new millennium, your future can glow brighter than sunshine.

"In 1991, at age 34," recalls Harold Sherman, a toy company executive with earnings in the mid-six-figure range, "my annual income was $32,000. That year I made a job change that boosted my earnings 30 percent. Since then, I have made additional changes that hiked me to my present level. And I'm not finished yet." His story is not uncommon.

"Prior to '91," Harold adds, "when dissatisfied with my career, I checked help wanted and job opportunity columns or contacted an employment agency. It didn't dawn on me in those days how limited access to the job market was. Today it's an entirely different ball game on a totally new playing field. Today, thanks to the computer and Internet, a greatly expanded marketplace is accessible to applicants and employers alike. What it boils down to," Harold says, "is that if you're under-appreciated, underpaid, and—*you are qualified*—you no longer have to settle, vegetate, or seethe. You can advance and grow—in your own organization or elsewhere. You can make it clear to your boss: 'If you want me and need me, pay the price.' "

But life is never that simple. Unprecedented economic and marketplace changes notwithstanding, some realities remain constant: To advance and grow you still have to SELL—your ideas and yourself. And you still have to COMPETE with those nasties who are trying to beat you out for the juiciest plums in the payroll department's fruit bin. You still need to develop successful strategies to tell one and all you refuse to be outsmarted.

The choice is yours. You can stand by on the sidelines while coworkers and associates snatch the choice assignments and win bonuses, raises, and promotions, or you can aggressively stir up the pot and bring yourself to the favorable attention of the powers that be.

Don't Type Yourself As a Runner-up

Winners win. Runners-up finish second, third, or last. If your supervisor, and *the supervisor's* boss, are savvy they probably have you pegged as either a potential winner or runner-up. Typically, their judgment is based on a combination of instinct, experience, and personal interaction, along with word-of-mouth and reported evaluation. Okay. The bad news is if you've been timid, passive, and wishy-washy in the past, you're not likely to rank high on Mr. or Ms. Big Shot's get-ahead list. The good news is that you can upgrade your ranking in no time flat by identifying your image-busting weaknesses and taking positive steps to flaunt your personal talents and capabilities. For an example, let's look at Anne McDonald.

Speak Up and Speak Out

■ Anne McDonald

Sometimes smart people do dumb things. Anne's IQ, when she was hired out of secretarial school, was a respectable 128. But by tracking her three-year career in the secretarial pool of the large, fast-growing insurance company that employed her, you wouldn't rate her as smart. Anne was a "poolie," which was not one of the plum jobs in her organization. Like other poolies she was assigned as needed to middle managers or supervisors who didn't rate high enough to warrant personal secretaries of their own. The choice "assistant-to" jobs were held by those with the title assistant-to high-level decision makers.

What frustrated Anne in particular was that she felt—no, more than felt, *knew*—she was at least as capable as Ellen, Bertha, Jeff, and others in her department who were aggressive and cagey enough to pick the plums from the corporate tree. *But just because they could do this didn't mean they were more qualified and competent than Anne.* Yet they were the winners, and she was the runner-up. Why?

Why? Posing this question to herself was the smartest thing Anne did in her three years with the company. The second smartest thing she did was to follow up on that question. During her assignments over the years, Anne had worked from time to time for Steve Merchant, a claims supervisor. In fact, whenever he could, Steve requested Anne specifically. A sharp and perceptive climber, he saw beyond her shyness and passivity to the bright, sensitive, and conscientious employee masked by the meek image she projected. Steve viewed Anne as creative, ethical, and dependable. He liked her as a person, and appreciated her competence as a worker.

Anne was in conflict with herself. Should she quit or stick it out? Her frustrations were getting her down. More than once she had been on the verge of resigning but an inner voice kept her from giving up too easily. Yet here she was on the verge again. Claire, executive secretary to Alan Jamison, a senior vice president, was opting for early retirement. The job, a super plum, was up for grabs, and Anne felt deep down that no one in the pool was better qualified than she. She also had heard via the grapevine that Valerie Emmet—conniving, outspoken Val—was pitching hard for the job and stood a good chance of getting it. If that happened, it was hard to determine who would be hurt more, Anne or Mr. Jamison. In Anne's view, if Val got the job it would be the final injustice.

She had never been closer to quitting. Anne made a courageous effort to swallow her pride. With the vibes good between them, she decided to confide her frustrations to Steve Merchant. "Stop me if I'm out of line. But you know what goes on around here. Maybe you can give me some advice."

The supervisor saw she was upset. Some people easily hide their emotions. Not Anne. Her feelings spilled out like milk from a broken container. Steve listened thoughtfully.

"Of course you're better qualified than Val. A hundred times better qualified. You'd be crazy to cop out."

"Do you really mean it?" she asked meekly.

"I wouldn't say it if I didn't mean it. Do me a favor. Compose a memo explaining why you're best qualified for the job. Lay it out like it is. Don't sell your qualifications short. In the meantime, I'll talk to Alan Jamison. I can't make any promises. But who knows, it might help."

It did help. That was two years ago. Anne won the appointment with a nice increase in pay thrown in. And she has earned two raises since with another one in the offing. All because when the time was right she spoke up and spoke out.

Ask Yourself the Crucial Question

Repeated surveys prove that the happiest and most satisfied workers are the men and women who strive for and achieve excellence. If you feel frustrated in your career, unappreciated and unrecognized, the crucial question to ask yourself is:

AM I DOING THE BEST JOB I POSSIBLY CAN?

People fail to do their best for a variety of reasons. If you are failing, the time is probably long overdue for you to pinpoint and ponder which of the following reasons are causing you to underperform.

- Your job bores you, and you feel it is not worth the effort.
- You aren't getting the information you need to do a good job.
- You lack the training and experience required.
- You're lazy; you lack ambition.
- You don't get along with your employer or supervisor.
- You don't get along with your coworkers.
- You feel there's no chance for advancement. Why knock yourself out?
- Your boss doesn't make it clear what she wants you to do.
- You feel you are overburdened with too much work.

Relate each of the above low-performance causes *honestly and objectively* to your personal experience on the job. Then, where applicable, determine—with as much help as you can get—what steps you can take to remedy the situation. The closing section of this chapter suggests that you discuss your future in—or outside of—your organization with a guru you can trust. If you feel you aren't performing to your full potential for one or more of the reasons listed above, this would be an excellent subject to bring up with your expert.

Adopt Courage As a Career Strategy

Winston Churchill stated the case simply enough: "Courage is the first of human qualities because it is the quality that guarantees all others."

In the previous story, job-frustrated Anne McDonald finally broke out of a blocked career to a happy and rewarding future because she summoned the courage to act positively and aggressively on behalf of herself.

We are all continuously afraid of one thing or another. Keep the following motto in mind and your career—and most other—problems will melt faster than an ice cube dropped on a steaming hot pavement.

ACHIEVING SUCCESS IN LIFE AND ON THE JOB IS A SIMPLE MATTER OF HAVING THE GUTS TO OVERCOME THE FEARS THAT BESET YOU.

Some typical fears:
◆ Jane is afraid of her autocratic and dictatorial boss who treats her unfairly.
◆ Bill received harsh criticism on an assigned project, and is afraid he will flop on the next project assigned.
◆ Frank is afraid the job he has been asked to tackle will be too tough for him.

- Alice is afraid that her profit improvement idea will be turned down by her boss.
- Beth is afraid that she won't be accepted by other members of the team to which she's been assigned.
- Jerry is afraid that Linda will win the promotion he seeks.
- Linda is afraid that if she gets the promotion she won't be able to handle the job.
- Mary is afraid she'll be bypassed for a merit increase.

And so on and so on. How many of these "shoes" fit your feet? What are you afraid of? More importantly, can you pinpoint and define the cause or causes of your fear? *Most* importantly, can you summon the courage to face up to your fear and take aggressive action to combat it?

Career specialist Lona O'Connor states in the Florida *Sun-Sentinel:* "You can go a long way toward learning courage if you find yourself a courage mentor—co-worker, manager, friend or family member." This person, she believes, will encourage you to make the most of your talents and capabilities, heat up your enthusiasm and feeling of self-worth, and at the same time suggest positive action to take in response to your fears.

DEVISE A STRATEGY TO HUMBLE YOUR COMPETITORS

The job or status you're after wouldn't be worth fighting for if others weren't hot on its trail as well.

Strategizing to beat the competition is simple if you ask the right questions. Say you have a particular job or assignment in mind. Do you have the know-how, training, savvy, and experience to han-

> "The job or status you're after wouldn't be worth fighting for if others weren't hot on its trail as well."

dle it? Can you handle it as well as or better than those competing against you? If your answer to these questions is yes, your course of action is clear: Work up a plan and go for it. How? The following pages will spell it out for you.

Or, suppose you're convinced that your paycheck is paltry. Or you're a woman earning less than a man who does the same job as you, but not half as well. What to do? Fight for what is rightfully yours with the tools this book will provide for you.

The key questions to focus on in these situations are: *How much are you worth to your boss? How much are you worth to your company?*

■ Bud and Brent

Bud Fowler, who had busted his butt for his bosses, pulled down $26,500 a year as assistant maintenance supervisor in an auto parts manufacturing plant. Brent Smith, his boss and department head, earned an annual income of $49,000. Bud knew as much as Brent and worked twice as hard. It wasn't fair, he decided. One day he worked up enough gumption to do something about it. He based his pitch for the income boost he had in mind on two facts of life as they pertained to his particular situation:

◆ Those working in jobs comparable to his at local competitive companies were paid more.

◆ His boss depended on him for the lion's share of supervisory work.

In a nutshell, Bud concluded he was worth substantially more than what he was getting. He knew, too, that his boss was a tough negotiator, and Bud anticipated that when he pitched for a raise Brent would probably offer him a token amount if anything. Bud had in mind a raise of four grand. Unrealistic? He didn't think so, but as a family man with a wife and three kids to support, he exercised caution. After checking the want ads and floating a few trial balloons, he felt the four grand was achievable. So he decided to shoot for $5,000.

It took courage to reach this conclusion, even more courage to approach Brent with it. Predictably, his boss hemmed and hawed, called his demands preposterous, and said he would try to get him $1,500. When Bud refused to back down, Brent said reluctantly, "Let me see what I can do."

The pitch Brent made to *his* boss was no less convincing than the one Bud had made to him. Bud Fowler knew he was worth the $4,000 and that's what he got.

Are you underpaid for the job you do? Are you *convinced* you're entitled to earn more? Is your conviction based on evidence backed by experience, know-how, training, and a realistic earnings comparison with other organizations in your area? Do you have the documentation to support your demand? If your answer to these questions is "yes," then ask yourself if you have the courage to stand up to your boss on a get-what-you-deserve-or-else basis? If you're unsure of the answer, give TV Anchor Katie Couric a call. Not so long ago the popular anchor's response to the above questions was a resounding **YES.** Sold on her worth, convinced that she was in a league with Tom Brokaw and other top anchors, she pitched NBC for the raise she deserved.

Do courage and conviction pay off? You decide. Underpaid at *$2 million a year* at the time, Katie more than tripled her earnings to $7 million. Katie is no more nor less human than you. If she can do it on her level, why not you on your level?

Selling Points

Selling yourself to your boss—or boss—has much in common with selling mangoes or mobile homes in the marketplace. As a sales rep in the field you have to present your product to buyers in its best possible light. You have to explain clearly how the item will be worth the price to the purchaser. Rules of salesmanship are the same whether the product is an automobile, insurance policy, can opener—or **YOU.**

Say your heart is set on a particular job. No matter who's trying to outsmart you, if you ask the following questions and come up with the right answers, you can't miss.

- Can you do the job without needing a lot of new training?
- Do you fit in as a member of the team?
- Did you evaluate yourself point by point against your competitors and come out on the plus side?
- Can you think creatively—"outside the box"—casting aside old restraints?
- Do your background and experience measure up to your boss's expectations?
- If you are rejected and decide to resign, how costly would it be for the company to hire and train a replacement? What bargaining chips do you have?
- How much of a hardship would your departure be for your boss?
- If you are accepted for the job, would the salary offered be in line with your requirements?
- Is your bid for the job timely?
- Finally, if your response to any of the above is negative, what steps can you take to overcome the inadequacy?

WHEN A COMPETITOR HITS BELOW THE BELT

Politics can pollute. Not only the government, but the workplace as well. Just as an elected official can't afford to ignore beltway politics, plant and office employees can't afford to disregard cronyism in the department or division.

■ Edith

Edith, a member of the systems group in a Chicago brokerage office, knew someone was undermining her position with Martha, her boss. She was pretty sure her adversary was Millie. During a break period Martha confided to a handful of key people, Edith included, that she was overworked and spreading herself too thin. "I have to delegate some of the special stuff I've been doing." She specified the Manley Report in particular as a time-consuming project. This report was a weekly analysis produced for Mr. Manley, a senior vice president.

Edith could handle the project with a minimum of turnover time and do it as well as anyone in the department. Getting the nod from Martha on the report would be the career break she'd been hoping for. But Edith was almost certain that Millie was working against her. Millie was no less hungry for the Manley Report than Edith.

When Edith's friend Linda confided some of Millie's dirty tricks to her, all doubts were removed. For example, Linda explained, Martha had heard via the grapevine that Millie had to take over a job because Edith was unable to handle it. There were implications of Edith's disloyalty and the rumor that a costly error had occurred because of "wrong information Edith had provided." And the story that she had left early when an urgently needed project was unfinished. A blatant lie.

What to do? Fight back, of course! Wheel out the howitzers. *But not blindly and mindlessly.*

Edith was mad enough to scream. If there is ever a time to count to 10, then do it once again backwards, it's when you're fist-fighting angry. On her computer Edith punched out a self-exonerating email to her boss. Dripping with rage, she accused Millie of unconscionably smearing her reputation and degrading the organization as well. It was probably true. But for one thing, Edith needed documentation. For another, action taken in the heat of anger rarely pays off. Added to that, email is anything but private and personal.

Edith's impulsive response was ill advised. Having been tossed off without adequate thought, the email was awkward and clumsily worded. It put her boss in a spot and embarrassed her. It took Edith down a peg or two in Martha's estimation. In the end, neither she nor Millie were assigned the project.

What *should* Edith have done under the circumstances? She would have been better served had she—before taking *any action*—taken the time to cool off and plan her counterattack. A better response may have been to approach a higher ranked confidant who was close to the boss, confide her dilemma, and ask for advice or for this person to intercede on her behalf. She might have requested a private meeting with Martha and, point by point, tried to persuade her that the charges against her were false and concocted by someone who was trying to hurt her.

SOMETIMES YOU CAN'T DO IT ALONE

Victor Hugo wrote, "Nothing is so powerful as an idea whose time has come."

But no one knows better than the top super-pros that even a great idea will bomb if it is not properly presented, promoted, and backed by the right influentials.

George's cost reduction plan was better than bright; it was brilliant. As a group leader in Billing, he was able to figure out it would save the company $250,000 a year. He had gone over the figures a dozen times. The plan meant a major undertaking, but he was certain the payoff would warrant it.

George could scarcely conceal his excitement. He looked forward to becoming an overnight hero. If he sold Mr. Henshaw on this idea it could be the break he'd been waiting for, leading to all kinds of advancement. Grabbing his rough notes, he made a beeline for his boss's office.

Question: *What's wrong with George's approach and follow-up action?*

Fortunately, on his way to the production manager's office, the young group leader ran into General Manager Wilbur Goss. "What's up, George? You look like you just won the lottery and are on your way to cash in the ticket."

"That's how I feel, sir." George gave Goss a capsulized rundown of the restructured billing system he had in mind.

The seasoned executive frowned. "The idea sounds good. But how much planning and preparation have you spent on the proposal?"

"What do you mean?"

"I'll be specific. Have you considered who in the company would benefit if your idea is accepted? And who might be hurt by it? In short, who might be for and against it? Before rushing pell-mell to blurt out your idea to Gus Henshaw, have you determined if the timing is right, if the company is in a position at this time to make the investment involved? Do you know if Henshaw can give your proposal the time and attention it deserves right now?

Can you cite other organizations that have installed the system successfully? Have you considered what the pitfalls and roadblocks might be?"

"Whew!" George blew out his breath. "Maybe I'd better put a little more thought into this undertaking."

The executive smiled. "Sounds like a good idea."

Great careers are built on good ideas. Suggestions for improvement are powerful tools that can help you beat out the competition for better jobs and better pay. But getting ideas is one thing, selling them another. George's idea might be good for the company, but not so good for some coworkers depending on individual situations. The restructuring might put a heavy work burden on Mary, or thin down Phil's work group and result in his loss of status. It could reflect badly on Tony who designed the system George plans to replace. Such possibilities must be taken into consideration.

> "Great careers are built on good ideas. But getting ideas is one thing, selling them another."

The workplace is a social environment. An old proverb states, "One hand washes another." That's why, if your goal is to get ahead on the job, it helps to cultivate a battalion of allies—coworkers at all levels who are rooting for you. Why are allies so important? Consider the following reasons:

- ◆ They are purveyors of information.
- ◆ They serve as links to key people you are trying to influence.
- ◆ They provide vocal support for your ideas and character.
- ◆ They offer critical judgments pro and con.
- ◆ Their backing adds weight and credibility to proposals you make.

◆ They offer the cooperation you need for ideas to succeed.

◆ They are your friends; they care about you.

What follows are some KEY WORDS to ponder. How many ring a bell with you in your workplace dealings? They work both ways when interacting with people:

Listening	**Enthusiasm**	**Contacts**
Networking	**Relationships**	**Mutual**
Supportive	**Reinforcement**	**Friendship**
Receptive	**Teamwork**	**Caring**
Cooperation	**Linking**	**Concern**

GET A LITTLE CHUTZPAH WORKING FOR YOU

Eager to get ahead and break out of your rut? Timidity may bring you sympathy, but it won't bring you success. *Chutzpah,* as defined in the Yiddish dictionary reads: Impudence, unmitigated gall, effrontery. We are not suggesting that you become rude and impertinent or an objectionable loudmouth. Such an image would demolish you.

But it's a fact of the competitive marketplace that the prize plums go to those bold and gutsy enough to stand out from the crowd, and sometimes that takes a little chutzpah.

In covering Steve Ballmer's appointment to the No. 2 spot at Microsoft by Microsoft's founder Bill Gates, *Newsweek*'s Steven Levy said, "In a company viewed as a legion of imperious eggheads, Ballmer's... the boisterous guy in a polo shirt who once shouted, 'Windows! Windows! Windows!' so loudly at a sales meeting that he hurt his vocal chords." Sometimes you have to raise your voice—and presence—above the crowd.

■ **Tess**

Tess, a junior accountant in the statistical department of a New York City department store, came up with a proposal that she calculated would make inventory taking more efficient and, at the same time, tighten security. When she pitched her idea at a meeting also attended by the financial vice president. Greg Saltzer, another accountant, made it sound like a hare-brained idea. When Greg made his points, his evidence was, in Tess's opinion, so inaccurate and blatantly wrong that it made her lips curl. Although normally meek, she rose and boldly accused Greg of gross and blatant misrepresentation and point by point rebutted his arguments. She knew this could either get the proposal approved or cost her her job.

The VP okayed the proposal. Tess won an increase in pay and was boosted a level in the organization. Greg won a reprimand.

IT'S NOT ENOUGH TO BE THE BEST PERSON FOR THE JOB

That's right, it's not enough to be best—you have to *prove* that you're best. Let's look at Scott's example.

■ **Scott**

When the foreman in a home appliances plant quit unexpectedly, his job was up for grabs. Scott, one of three assistants, could almost taste the promotion and juicy wage hike it would bring. But that sweet taste turned sour when Jo Ann beat him to the punch. Her MEMO TO MANAGEMENT was headed: "What I Would Do to Make the Department More Profitable," and subtitled: "Why

I Should Be Given the Chance." Her well thought-out ideas were detailed step by step.

Scott's potential was equally impressive. Yet the other guy won out. Why? Because Scott was passive in contrast to Jo Ann's smart, timely, aggressive response. JoAnn worked so quickly, in fact, that Scott was left at the starting line.

CONVINCE THE BOSS YOU CAN DO IT

Repeated surveys show that most managers are poor delegators. There are several reasons for this. A manager may feel a task is confidential and can't be reassigned. Many cling to long-held projects from habit. And some managers think the job's too important or complicated for a lesser mortal to handle. Or from sheer force of habit. However, this can work to an ambitious employee's advantage, as Irene shrewdly discovered. Her career objective was to win a promotion from Grade II Staff Professional to Grade I. An opening in Grade I came up for grabs. The move would mean a 15 percent wage boost for Irene plus an important step up the ladder to her ultimate goal as a salaried rather than hourly employee.

The question was: How could she swing it?

Irene racked her brain and recalled she had read somewhere that **"if you want to succeed, identify your boss's most critical needs and take steps to fulfill them."**

At least one of her boss's most critical needs was easy to pinpoint. Mr. Seymour usually put in 10 to 12 hours a day. Almost invariably, after everyone else had gone home, he was still grinding away at his desk. Mr. Seymour was spreading himself too thin. How, Irene wondered, could she use this to her benefit?

Irene thought of the *Weekly Productivity Report!* and an idea hit her like an inspiration from Valhalla. Writing the report took four or more hours to complete per week. If she could relieve him of this duty it would ease his burden considerably.

She most certainly could, Irene decided.

It was a complicated report. Irene knew she could do it, but she would have to work fast before one of her coworkers, Tom and Alice, preempted her. Approaching her boss, she said boldly, "Mr. Seymour, I've been studying the *Weekly Productivity Report.* If you could spare an hour of break-in time, I know I could handle it."

Her boss raised his eyebrows. "Do you really think so?"

"I don't think so; *I know so.*"

You probably predicted the ending. Today Grade I Irene expertly completes the *Weekly Productivity Report*—and has gone up a sizable notch in Mr. Seymour's estimation.

Whether your boss is receptive to change or not, it takes a well-considered game plan to achieve the goal you desire.

Step 1: Pinpoint the need.
Step 2: Persuade your boss you can take care of it.
Step 3: Make sure the timing is right.
Step 4: Anticipate and prepare for objections.
Step 5: Act boldly and swiftly, before someone else beats you to the punch.

WHEN IN DOUBT, CONSULT A GURU

■ John's dilemma

John, 37, credit manager for a furniture company, earned a respectable paycheck each week. Still, he was planted squarely on the horns of a dilemma: To resign or stay?

The questions John posed to himself were intriguing:

◆ Could he earn as much or more doing the same job elsewhere? *Doubtful.*

◆ Would his opportunity for growth be as good? *Questionable.*

◆ Would his boss honor his promise made several months ago to make him a vice president? *Maybe.*

◆ Would the company's plans to expand come to pass? *Unlikely.*

◆ Would his opportunity to learn more be greater in another company? *Probably.*

◆ Would his rapport with other key players be as good? *Why not? He was well liked.*

◆ Did he enjoy going to work in the morning? *Not particularly.*

So, where could John go from there? He was advised to consult a guru. Good advice.

John's uncle was a partner in a nationally known consulting firm. If anyone was qualified to help as a guru, it was Uncle Mort. When he saw the anxious look on his nephew's face he asked the question he posed over and over to clients: "What's the problem?"

John spelled it out as clearly as he could. Uncle Mort grinned. "Piece of cake."

"Sure, you're not the one in my spot."

"Suppose I was? What would I do?"

John waited.

"The solution is so simple and old-fashioned I'm almost ashamed to suggest it. I would take a blank sheet of paper, draw a line down the middle, head the left side 'pro' and the right side 'con.' I would then list in the appropriate columns what you like about your job and what you don't like. Finally, I would assign a weight to each pro and each con. Then I would tally them up and make my decision."

With Uncle Mort's help that's exactly what John did. That was a year ago. Within two months John had changed jobs. His earnings declined for a while. But the situation is steadily improving. He is learning sophisticated new computer software and network configurations, expects to equal his previous earnings before long, and, most importantly, in the morning he can't wait to get to the office.

Get It Down In Black and White

Hopefully, you're as good as your word. Unfortunately, not everyone is. Consider Ethel and her dilemma.

■ Ethel

Ethel, executive secretary to a bank's loan officer, one day found herself in the same dilemma as John. She could either hang around or seek greener pastures. Her career goal was being promoted to financial assistant, having increased status, and getting the earnings boost that would go with it. The question: Was it in the cards or not?

Ethel confronted Mr. Green, her boss, who assured her the promotion was definitely in the cards.

"When?"

Her boss frowned. On the one hand, Ethel was a valued employee; on the other, he didn't care for the question. "I can't make a snap judgment."

Ethel already had decided that either she would get what she wanted or say goodbye. She got this message across to Mr. Green. Pressed, he promised her the assistant title and wage increase within six months.

Ethel waited, not too patiently, for the six months to expire. When it did, she confronted Mr. Green again, who seemed to have a problem recollecting that he had made the promise. "Be patient," he advised, "it will come."

When the promotion didn't come, Ethel went. She had learned a lesson she would never forget, that is, get it in writing!.

Tip: In planning your future, be sure to get any verbal commitment converted to writing. Create documentation to support any discussion held or agreements reached.

CHAPTER LESSONS

✓ Speak up. To advance and grow—no matter the job market—you will always need to sell your accomplishments, skills, and ideas to your future or present employer.

✓ You also will always have to compete with coworkers for the best job assignments, promotions, and pay raises. Move boldly and quickly but with well thought-out plans.

✓ Strive for excellence in everything that you do. Ask yourself if you are doing the best you can. If you are not, ask yourself why and find ways to improve. Confront your fears.

✓ Cultivate allies in the workplace. They can provide you with information and knowledge; introduce you to people that can help you move up; offer constructive criticism of your ideas; help you as part of a team; and, most importantly, be your friends.

✓ Adopt courage as a career strategy. Find yourself a Courage-Mentor who will help you to recognize your talents and abilities, gain enthusiasm and self-respect, and learn how to overcome the fears that are holding you back in your career.

✓ Get any negotiated agreements in writing!

HOW DO YOU FIT IN? THE AUTHOR'S REMINISCENCE

In my 10 years with Faberge Perfumes Inc., I advanced from supervisory rank to director of systems, a key management job. In my 40s, I grew increasingly restless. It wasn't what I wanted to do. I didn't like supervising a lot of people. I'm not a techie by nature. I already had written and sold articles to management and general publications, and I had won a contract for a book. I felt I could make it as a writer.

I got along well with my boss, Philip Brass, the company's executive vice president. He had high regard for me, largely because of my frequent suggestions for improvements which I wrote in memo form. An aspiring writer, I seized every opportunity to write. Time and again I half-decided to resign and write full time. For three years running I requested—virtually demanded—a preposterous raise, and each time, I got it, to my amazement.

I finally decided it was now or never and gave Phil a month's notice. He was stunned when I told him what I wanted to do. "You're making an awful mistake," he cautioned. He described the opportunities I'd be foregoing. "You could become controller of this company, even financial vice president."

Phil was one of the best managers I ever knew, a decent and compassionate human being. But he didn't view my career ambitions from my perspective. He didn't understand that from my point of view, promotion to financial vice president would have been a disaster, nothing short of a nightmare.

Like so many high-level executives, Phil was too busy to soul search and really get to know his key people. I held fast to my resolve to resign. It was one of the best decisions I ever made. As these words are being written, my latest book, *Achieving Financial Independence As a Freelance Writer,* is being published. The truth is that, no matter how well I did on the job, I wasn't functioning at my best and reaching my potential as I saw it.

It's a crucial point to consider. Before struggling and battling to win that key job on which your sights are set, ask yourself: Do you really want it? Do you fit? If the answer is "no" it may be time for a change.

CHAPTER 4:
THE KNOWLEDGE LOOP

Problem: You Are Out of the Knowledge Loop
Rx: Learn How To Get the Dope Fast

A prudent question is one-half of wisdom.
—Francis Bacon, Author and Philosopher

Penny, a group leader, was uncertain about the proposed billing system at her company. She had reservations but couldn't explain her concerns. Arlene, another group leader, was enthusiastic about the proposal and made no effort to hide it.

At a special meeting, the division head probed his key people's feelings.

"Penny, why are you opposed to the system?"

Penny frowned. "I'm not exactly opposed," she wavered. "I just feel we could do with more study."

The VP turned to Arlene who said, "I think the sooner we get going, the better. I've been looking into this setup. Two of our competitors are already on line with the system. They cut order processing time 30 percent and also boosted productivity." She handed the VP a printout. "The facts and figures in this report speak for themselves."

The executive scanned the report. "Let's do it," he said. "Arlene, I want you to head up this project."

No question about it. The more you know—*and the more you show what you know*—the more you grow. This is no new revelation. Confucius said it centuries ago: "The essence of knowledge is, having it, to apply it; not having it, to confess your ignorance."

WHEN YOU ARE NEW ON THE JOB

Whatever your IQ, whatever your formal educational background, when you are new on the job you're a dummy. You're unfamiliar with the organization, with its motivations and goals, with the methods and procedures in use. Your job description isn't as clear as you would like it to be. Your boss is an unknown factor, his or her expectations uncertain. Same thing for your coworkers.

Management consultant Alston Caldwell states the case: "When you are new at the job you are out of the Knowledge Loop. It could take weeks or months to get both your feet on the ground."

When job advancement and increased pay are your goals, the Knowledge Loop extends to a number of areas. You will need to know:

◆ Your organization—its plans, directions, and goals.
◆ The role of your department and work group in achieving its goals.
◆ How and where you, specifically, fit into the picture.
◆ Your performance expectations.
◆ The technical aspects of your work.
◆ Where—and to whom—you must go to access information.
◆ The computer's role in fulfilling your job more effectively.
◆ The opportunities available to continue your training.
◆ Your opportunities for advancement and growth.
◆ Whom to ask for help when you have a tough problem to solve or a decision to make.
◆ Compensation. Find out if you can, via the grapevine or otherwise, how much coworkers, male and female, are paid—*especially coworkers who do the same job as you.*

Most importantly, you will have to know yourself. What are your personal desires and needs as they affect your life and career goals? How much are you willing to sacrifice to achieve your objectives? How important is money in your scheme of things?

Find Yourself a Mentor

In this New Economy, an increasing number of organizations are installing mentor programs. Such programs are especially useful in keeping newer employees satisfied and making them more effective in the workplace. The best advice we can offer:

If a mentor system exists take advantage of it. If no formal system exists, find a mentor on your own. Look for an experienced sympathetic executive who has the savvy and sensitivity to provide the counsel you need.

■ **Bernice**

Bernice was bright and ambitious. She was a business administration major and ranked among the top 20 percent of her class. After she was interviewed as a senior at New York University, she was one of three candidates hired by a large health products company. She was indoctrinated into the marketing department where she was enrolled in a three-month training program. Her progress was impressive. Among other favorable comments she received, her evaluation stated, "shows good promotion potential."

Following the program's completion she was assigned to work with Lois, a marketing supervisor and project leader in her 50s, a veteran employee who had more than 15 years' experience with the company. Lois's chief responsibility was customer service. Her group consisted of six people including herself. Bernice's job title was Customer Service Correspondent. She was assigned to an alcove equipped with a new computer with the latest software and high-speed Internet access.

The elements of communication in general and customer correspondence in particular were stressed in the training program. This was all well and good. Bernice had a PC at home and had taken courses in college on Windows, word processing programs, the Internet, and other aspects of computer technology. She had been using email extensively for more than two years.

Bernice had a natural sensitivity to customer needs. In both the company's training program and her college classes the critical importance of customer satisfaction to the bottom line had been stressed again and again. Despite her supervisor's long experience, Bernice felt that Lois's sensitivity did not match her own. Her boss was a dedicated email advocate. She insisted that, where applicable, it was the fastest and most efficient way to respond to customer inquiries and complaints. The alternative and less preferable method, she instructed subordinates, was to use conventional mail, or "snail mail."

Bernice agreed with her boss up to a point. But she also thought that in some cases, such as when the customer was particularly upset or needed critical health information, the most effective response was a phone call. Calls took more time and were more expensive than email or snail mail. But where personalized attention could mollify an unhappy customer and, hopefully, save the account or help solve a health problem, the cost was worth it. But, after all, Lois was her boss. If Lois instructed her to use email, then it was her responsibility to comply even if she didn't agree. Or was it?

Lois was pleasant enough, but she was rigid in her demands. Bernice didn't feel friction between them—well, not exactly. But Lois's rules annoyed her at times. For one thing, Bernice had acquired a particular expertise with regard to a specific category of health products. She rightly felt that no one was better qualified to handle communications related to these products than she. When she mentioned that to Lois, her boss thanked her for the comment and said she would think about it. But that's the last Bernice heard of it. Her annoyance was changing into frustration.

Finally, now almost six months on the job, she recalled a section in the policy manual that described the company's mentor system that was just getting under way. Employees who needed help in solving problems and making decisions were encouraged under the system to contact an executive mentor for guidance. A list of names was included for different departments and disciplines.

Bernice telephoned Anita Lewis, a suggested mentor assigned to her department. Ms. Lewis, a Vice President, arranged for a confidential interview the following day. She was friendly, discreet, experienced, and, most importantly, understanding of and sympathetic to Bernice's growing frustrations. "Thank you for coming to me," she said. "This will require some thought, but don't worry, we'll work it out." And they did.

ARE YOU REALLY UNDERPAID?

Survey after survey reports that in industry after industry women's salaries are significantly lower than those of men who do the same jobs. In fields from accounting and banking to health care and financial management, men earn 20 to 30 percent more then women counterparts. In sales—real estate, insurance, and advertising—the same disparity exists. (For information

SALARIES FOR MEN AND WOMEN BY EDUCATION LEVEL

EDUCATION LEVEL	MEN	WOMEN
Bachelor's degree	$62,543	$40,263
Master's degree	$75,441	$49,635
Professional degree	$130,711	$58,540
PhD	$107,988	$38,903

Source: Money Income in the United States, U.S. Census Bureau

on salary disparities between men and women based on education levels, see the chart above.)

In many companies, salaries of employees are held by management to be confidential. The reason is clear. If you work alongside Jim, Joan, or Hank and do the same work they do for 15 or 20 percent less money, the inevitable question, voiced or unvoiced, will be: "Why is my income lower than theirs?"

So let's say you come up with a reasonable answer. Jim's seniority exceeds yours. Joan's performance is clearly superior. Hank works a less desirable shift. You can live with that. But what if such disparities don't exist? Suppose Jim is paid more because he's the boss's nephew. Or suppose Joan is engaged in an illicit affair with her supervisor. Or suppose Hank is the boss's longtime bowling partner. Or your supervisor doesn't like your looks, the color of your skin, your religion or ethnicity, your political preferences, or your age.... In such cases your sense of injustice could rightly flare like a July Fourth Roman candle. A fixation may enter your head: What action can I take to get my paycheck equalized? If you have an actual case of injustice and want to change it, good for you. Righteous dissatisfaction is the first step toward self-improvement. No one will take up your cause if you don't do it yourself.

The point makes itself. Too many bosses act annoyed when employees think of ways to better their positions. Bosses yearn for peaceful, productive environments. To state it bluntly, in some employers' perception it is not in their best interest for employees to be able to draw a comparison between their own salaries and those of their coworkers—or between their wages and those paid by competitors.

> "But as an employee it is in your best interest to . . . make sure you are paid a fair day's wage for an honest day's work."

But as an employee it is in *your* best interest to be able to make that comparison and to make sure you are paid a fair day's wage for an honest day's work. Thus, keeping inside the Knowledge Loop also means being in a position to compare your own compensation against those of the rest of the field inside and outside of the company.

We know of one case where a qualified engineer, a veteran employee in his late 30s, was shocked to learn that a counterpart working for a competitor across town earned 40 percent more than he did. His company's "confidentiality" policy specified that "anyone who disclosed a salaried employee's wages to others would be subject to dismissal." Although he had been insecure and wavering in the past, that engineer was emboldened to find a job elsewhere. He was gone so fast, the dust hardly settled before his boss realized he had left. Good for him! But he could have done it *years ago*. His failure to keep abreast of compensation in his field cost him thousands of dollars, not to mention months of personal growth and development.

■ Tina's Dilemma

The worst kind of job is the one where you are angry about an injustice, real or imagined. This is the kind of situation where you keep simmering until frustration sets in. Once bitterness gains a foothold, it messes up not only your career but also your emotional well being. The injustice bugging Tina was not imagined. Executive aides in the greeting card manufacturing company where she was a three-year employee broke down into three categories: Administrative Assistant, Executive Secretary, and Secretary.

> "Once bitterness gains a foothold, it messes up not only your career but also your emotional well being."

Tina's job description and title read "Secretary." The work she did 90 percent of the time matched the job description for Executive Secretary, and in some instances Administrative Assistant. It was not a large company. All six Administrative Assistants were male. Ditto for five of seven Executive Secretaries. All eight Secretaries in the secretarial pool were women. Tina, an African American woman, appeared to be stuck where she was.

What really irritated Tina was that the ineffective Bradley J. was solidly entrenched as Executive Secretary to Mr. Pollimer. Without going into detail, suffice it to say that Brad was qualified according to the stipulations and requirements of his job description *up to a point.* Beyond that point, if Brad couldn't handle the task or project it was usually turned over by Mr. Pollimer to Tina. Mr. Pollimer was as generous with flattery as he was stingy with money and meaningful recognition. Brad's salary was 40 percent higher than Tina's. Perhaps a good match since he was only 40 percent as effective.

Over the months Tina's repeated complaints and appeals to Mr. Pollimer and other executives were met with sympathetic suggestions to be patient. She did receive one token pay increase and a paltry "bonus."

One day as she was browsing the Internet, Tina came across news from Washington of the president's initiative to enforce and bolster the Equal Pay Act, which, according to the National Committee on Pay Equity "...prohibits discrimination in compensation for 'equal work' on the basis of sex..." and, as stated in Title VII of the Civil Rights Act of 1964 " ... prohibits discrimination in compensation because of race, color, religion, national origin, and/or sex."

Tina took a deep breath, downloaded the article, and marched with it into Mr. Pollimer's office. She told him how much she liked the company, enjoyed her work, and appreciated his confidence in her ability. She added meekly, "I would sure hate to sue this company on the basis of discrimination." Today at last, Tina's desk hosts a plaque that reads Executive Secretary.

Morals of the Story: 1. Find out what you're entitled to. 2. Devise an effective way to get it. 3. Then act on your plan.

IF YOU DON'T KNOW, ASK!

Murray K. was proud of himself. He had beat out a half dozen other candidates to land the data processing job. And he deserved it. He had excelled in his previous job at a laundry products company, he had demonstrated his expertise. He would do well here too; his confidence level had been high. Had been! But the initial weeks with his new employer, an industrial paints distributor, had him sweating. No two companies are alike. The paint business is a far cry from the laundry products business. Data processing is a complex field. His new employer's way of doing things was different from what Murray had been accustomed to. He no longer felt like an expert. His self-esteem was eroding, his self-image tarnishing. Most importantly, he felt that his boss was beginning to have doubts about him. Had hiring this guy been a good choice? Murray was worried he might not survive his probationary period.

> "Don't be afraid to ask questions when you don't have an answer."

Three weeks into the new job he was assigned a special report to prepare. The further he got into it, the more worried he became. He had questions about a number of aspects but decided to keep his mouth shut. He didn't want to look like a dummy. Murray tried to be philosophical. He would do the best he could do, let the chips fall where they may. When he turned in the report to his supervisor, Mr. Gordon instructed him to have a seat while he looked over it. His boss's frown deepened as he scrolled down the figures. Finally, he laid down the report on his desk. From the look on his face, Murray figured this was it. I'm out of here, he thought.

His boss shook his head. "Murray, this report isn't worth the paper it's printed on. You used gross sales instead of net. You did an annual comparison of commissions instead of quarterly."

Murray replied miserably, "I wasn't sure about those figures."

Mr. Gordon closed his eyes as if in prayer. "For the love of God, if you weren't sure, why didn't you ask?"

The unhappy young recruit lowered his eyes. "I guess I didn't want to look stupid."

> "Knowing how and when to ask the right question is a major career-building skill."

"Murray, what makes people look stupid isn't *asking* a question when they're not sure, it's *failing to ask*. You were selected for this job from a field of candidates because of your record and reputation. It was assumed you had knowledge or were capable of acquiring it. The single most powerful tool I know of for filling in knowledge gaps is a questioning mind. *Never,* and I mean *never,* resort to guesswork when you're not sure of the answer. Now re-do this report, and when you don't know, ask." This was an admonition Murray never forgot.

Are You a Skilled Interrogator?

Knowing how and when to ask the right question is a major career-building skill. It enhances your ability to make sound decisions and solve difficult problems. Actually, asking the right question is more than a skill, it's an art. How do you rate as an investigative reporter? Let's find out. Take the following quiz as objectively as possible, then score yourself at the end.

(Note: If you do not own this copy of Job Smarts, *then be sure to make a photocopy of this quiz before you mark your answers.)*

	YES	NO
1. Is it your policy to never guess at an answer?	___	___
2. Do you honestly admit it when you don't know the answer?	___	___
3. Do you think twice before asking a question?	___	___
4. Do you have access to people whose answers you trust?	___	___
5. Do you persist if the answer you get isn't clear?	___	___
6. If the question is important, do you double-check the answer?	___	___
7. Do you consider the respondent's motive in supplying the answer?	___	___
8. Do you organize important questions carefully?	___	___
9. Are you reliable in supplying answers to questions?	___	___
10. Do you question an answer if you suspect it's not right?	___	___
11. Do you probe further if you don't understand the answer?	___	___
12. Do you encourage people to ask you questions?	___	___
13. Do you never laugh at a question no matter how silly it seems?	___	___
14. Do you record answers to vital questions so you won't forget them?	___	___
15. Do you invite feedback when explaining a project or task?	___	___

Rate Yourself

The *yeas* have it! Score 10 for each YES answer. If you responded honestly and objectively to this quiz, 150 qualifies you as a charter member of the Exclusive Q+ Club. A rating of 130 entitles you to Honorable Mention. Any score lower than this means you have a bit of intensive soul-searching to do.

Total _____

ARE YOU COMPUTER-SAVVY OR ONLY HALFWAY THERE?

An ad placed by the *Washington Post* states that 1,789,000 people read the *Post* daily. Of this number, 1,699,999 complain about their jobs. Additionally, 250,000 have used a computer. Only 10,000 have used it for something other than computer games.

Considering that with the right hardware and software you can go anywhere, this should give you something to think about.

When your career ship pulls in, will you be prepared to step aboard or get left at the dock? More and more in the months ahead, the answer to this question will depend on the level of computer expertise you possess. School training is just one important piece of your career preparation pie. Owning a PC and aggressively experimenting with it and exploring its possibilities is another important career-prep piece, and it is the best career-boosting investment you could make. For many, on-the-job computer training is the most significant piece of all. The more computer gurus you have access to and work with or for, the faster your technical expertise will grow.

Paul Henderson, a Software Development Manager for Microsoft and, as of this writing, President of BAM (Blacks at Microsoft), is a highly successful executive in the computer know. One of the great career advantages Paul enjoys is the privilege of working with a team of people who are among the nation's most computer literate.

He says, "The magnitude of knowledge here is incredible. There's nothing like being able to . . . actually talk to the person who's writing the code. If you want to get something done and need help, you can get someone out there who's already done it and find the help you need. There's just a wealth of knowledge here to call on."

A wealth of knowledge to call on is money in anyone's bank, assuming of course that you are willing to make a withdrawal. Are you a member of the vast army of employees who feel underappreciated and underpaid? Don't underestimate the career-boosting opportunity of working with computer-savvy associates. Sharpen your computer expertise to meet the demands of the Information Age and you won't be underpaid for long.

■ How Alice Missed the Boat

Two years ago, after earning their high school diplomas, Alice and her friend Jennifer enrolled in a program of computer courses offered at a respected vocational school. They completed the program successfully and set out job hunting together. Both of the young women's IQs were higher than average. Their personalities sparkled. They were offered entry-level trainee jobs at a local insurance company.

> "Sharpen your computer expertise to the demands of the Information Age and you won't be underpaid for long."

The personnel manager said, "The PCs we use here are IBM clones. At the end of three months, if you are qualified to work with Word and Quicken, you will be taken off trainee status, be removed from probation, and be put on the permanent payroll. How does that sound?"

Jennifer responded enthusiastically and was immediately hired. Alice appeared skeptical.

"What's the problem?" the personnel manager asked.

"I was trained on a MAC; I never used a PC."

"That shouldn't be too much of a problem. The training program will cover it."

Alice's face still registered doubt. "I don't know . . . "

"Well, maybe you're right," the manager cut in. "I'm sure you will find something where you will be more comfortable."

Alice did find a job where the computers in use were MACs. The job required less training, and Alice quickly settled into a comfortable groove. But that's where she stayed. Her job may be easier, but today Jennifer earns 30 percent more than her friend and enjoys a prestigious title—all because she was smart enough to understand that training is indeed "money in the bank."

> "The biggest mistake you could make . . . is to draw the conclusion that high tech is not your cup of tea."

Moral of the story: In the Information Age, the biggest mistake you could make when building career skills is to draw the conclusion that high tech is not your cup of tea. True, it can be complex. It can be involved. *But this is only until training simplifies it.* Take a tip from the top pros in almost any field you can name: Seize every opportunity you can for as much technical instruction as you can get.

Good Fun vs. Hard Work

There's much to be said for both. But whoever said you can't have both? South Florida education executive Robert E. Levinson states the case: "Experience proves time and again that nothing is more certain than hard work to lead to good fun, with self-esteem and self-satisfaction as byproducts. In fact, the more you learn about a subject, the more you come to enjoy it."

Does hard work lead to good fun? If you're not sure, ask hard-working Vanessa Sloat, a recent graduate of the University of Miami law school. She was recruited as a senior by the West Palm Beach law firm of Akerman Senterfitt for the position of first-year associate, with a salary of $74,000. But Vanessa also received a $31,000 raise before even starting her job. For $105,000 plus bonus, you can have a carload of fun.

Or ask John Weiss III, who graduated with top honors from Florida International University's e-commerce MBA program. John considered job offers as high as $150,000 from tech giants Motorola and Intel before settling in at a Miami Beach Internet start-up.

We concede these are examples of extreme salaries. But as Florida *Sun-Sentinel* business writer Joan Fleischer Tamen points out, "With a booming economy and ever-tightening labor market, employers are anxiously recruiting students with job offers topping $50,000 and benefits that include signing bonuses, options, and tuition for graduate school." Starting salaries for tech and science grads top the list. According to a 2001 survey by the National Association of Colleges and Employers, grads with chemical engineering degrees are starting at $48,890; computer engineering, $53,443; electrical engineering, $50,850; and information science and systems $44,251.

No question about it. Excelling in these fields represents a carload of bust-a-gut time. But as Robert Levinson points out, the rewards are well worth it. We think it may be a good idea to consider a strategy employed by marketing executives nationwide. In an effort to motivate sales personnel to work harder to bring in more orders and open new accounts, sales contests are run with heady awards for top performers. These awards range from new cars to exotic vacations. Salespeople are given slick photos of Hawaiian beach sites or a shiny new vehicle to keep close at hand to whet their appetites. And experience shows that this "award ploy" works. One winning rep says, "More often than I can recall, when, tempted to knock off early as opposed to putting in an extra hour or two, a hungry look at that Camry kept my nose to the grindstone."

As a young person on the way up, you can apply the same self-motivational psychology. Suppose, for example, you are a high school or college student, or a recent grad considering further education, and you have the tough question facing you: Should I sign up for advanced studies (while working or not) or opt for an easier life? Why not draw up a chart for yourself highlighting the salaries currently being offered to job applicants with masters' and doctors' degrees. Keeping such a chart close at hand, and drawing a comparison between what your career and earnings potential might be with and without those credentials might give you something to shoot for and think about.

BLUE-COLLAR WORKERS IN THE INFORMATION AGE

Okay! So you've had it with formal education. You are a high school grad, or even a drop-out and you decided you put in all the classroom time you intend to. That's your privilege. It's your life, your call. No one has the right to force-feed you. But does that mean you are beyond hope, destined to be underpaid and frustrated for years to come? No way! Not if you play your technical cards right.

■ Charley's New Career

Charley B. was never much of a student. Except for shop, math, and mechanical drawing, he had just barely managed to squeak out a high school diploma. Predictably, when he shopped the job market for work, he was turned down repeatedly for the well-paying positions because of his poor showing in school and lack of a college degree. So he wound up hustling cases and cartons at Kmart until his friend Ernie got on his back.

Ernie, who had dropped out of high school after two years, earned $30,000 a year repairing equipment in the maintenance department of a manufacturing company.

Shooting straight from the hip, Ernie declared, "Charley, you're sick!"

"What do you mean by that?" Charley snapped back.

"Settling for peanuts when you could be making good money."

"Yeah, how? With my crummy marks and no college degree?"

"Charley, you're good with your hands. When your Uncle Pete's fancy work station was delivered, you assembled it in no time flat when no one else could. You can take a car's engine apart and put it together again without breaking a sweat."

Charley nodded despondently. "I tried for an auto mechanic's job around town, but they want work experience."

"Yeah, that figures. Okay, why not go into business for yourself like my cousin Lou in Ohio did three years ago. He placed ads in the local papers and started out repairing cars in his backyard. He's a good mechanic, honest, and his rates are cheap because he has low overhead. The word spread like wildfire and so did his reputation. Today he's earning good money and has two guys handling the overflow."

The idea sounded interesting to Charley and he decided to give it a try. He placed a couple of ads in the paper and work began dribbling in. He didn't quit his job until he started to build up a following. At last word he's more than equaling his wages at Kmart and his business is growing. He loves the work and the idea that he is now an entrepreneur. And incidentally, he's back at school—at least part time—taking advanced auto repair courses at the local vocational school. Another discovery Charley made is that classrooms aren't the only source of continuing education. As author John Kieran wrote: "I am a part of everything I have read." Charley devours every book or magazine article on automotive repair he can get his hands on. The demand for his service continues to grow now that he is well inside the Knowledge Loop.

> "Opportunities abound. All it takes is the moxie and initiative to seek them out."

Good jobs for young people who skip college or drop out of high school are fading faster than blue denims in the hot sun. But as the economy changes, a demand for technical expertise—mechanical, electronic, and a host of specialized niches—continues to grow. Opportunities abound. All it takes is the moxie and initiative to seek them out.

DON'T LET YOUR JOB DESCRIPTION CONFINE YOU

As a member of the plant engineering department, Burt's job description fell under the title Service Equipment Mechanic—Grade II. Among other responsibilities he was required, *under a supervisor's direction,* to use prints and diagrams to maintain, repair, and monitor environmental and processing systems.

> "Ambitious goals are not simply fulfilled; you have to plan in order to meet them."

He had to monitor system controls and regulators by periodically checking gauges and thermostats. He was required to perform sprinkler and heating unit tests. He was expected to troubleshoot problems with air, hot water, hydraulic, and other equipment, again *under supervisory assistance and guidance*. And it was part of his job to make sure the plant was in compliance with safety and housekeeping rules.

Burt was ambitious. After a year on the job his sights were set on the next step up the company ladder, Service Equipment Mechanic—Grade I. This would mean a significant boost in both his status and pay. It would also represent another step closer to his ultimate goal of becoming department head. As a Grade I he would obviously need to understand Grade II assignments and supervise Grade II workers. Plus a whole lot more.

Ambitious goals are not simply fulfilled; you have to plan in order to meet them. Toward this end, Burt had a five-step program in mind:

1. Prove himself to be an outstanding team member and excel at his job.
2. Determine what additional skills he would need for a promotion to Grade I.
3. Make it his business to learn and master these skills.
4. Seize every opportunity to display his newly acquired knowledge.
5. Adhere to his Grade II job description within reason without being hog-tied by its provisions.

Burt worked hard for weeks to carry his plan to fruition. Having fulfilled steps one through three to his satisfaction, he decided it was time to focus hard on steps four and five. He thus took advantage of every opportunity he could to convince his boss that he was ready for promotion. This was when step 5 came into play. It was time to deviate strategically from the strictures of his job description that required him to complete specific assignments under supervisory assistance and guidance.

Occasions soon presented themselves. More than once, when his boss was not on hand, Burt completed a job on his own. Although the Grade II job description said it was beyond his scope to do so, he isolated malfunctioning components on his own. Burt was confident in his knowledge and judgement. More than once, he spotted potentially hazardous conditions and came up with ways to eliminate them, which was another specific Grade I responsibility.

At the outset Burt's boss raised a wary eyebrow when confronted with his bold initiatives. But one by one, as he began to realize that Burt knew what he was doing, that his initiatives worked, and, most importantly, *that they made his own job easier,* he not only accepted the initiatives but threw advanced work Burt's way. In time, when a Grade I job opened up, who do you think was selected for it?

Moral of the story: Don't allow yourself to be restrained and constricted by your job description. It's not enough to be within the Knowledge Loop; it is equally important to demonstrate how darned good you are to the powers that be.

CHAPTER LESSONS

✓ The more you know—and the more you show you know—the more you grow.

✓ We're all "dummies" when we are new to a job. But smart employees don't stay dumb for long. As quickly as possible, they learn the ins and outs of their job, the goals of the organization, who to go to for key information, and other important factors at play in their work environment. Those are the employees who soon get noticed and promoted.

✓ Find yourself a mentor who can advise and educate you—and help you to advance your career.

✓ Part of the Knowledge Loop includes knowing what others doing the same job are paid and calculating how much pay you deserve. The more deeply you become entrenched in the Knowledge Loop, the faster and higher you will climb.

✓ Don't be afraid to ask questions. The only stupid question is the one that is not asked. Asking questions—and not guessing—will help you to avoid problems and feel the disappointment of your boss down the road.

✓ Know when and how to ask the right questions. This will help you to make better decisions and solve problems faster.

✓ Become computer literate. Learn as much as you can about computers and computer hardware and software from books, the Internet, family, friends, coworkers, and hands-on experience.

✓ Not all good jobs require a bachelor's degree. There is a growing demand for workers with technical expertise in computer science, mechanics, and electronics—jobs that usually require an associate's degree or less.

✓ Don't be constrained by your job title. Plan for your career goals and stay in the Knowledge Loop so that you will be able to advance to the next rung on the career ladder.

CHAPTER 5:
LEARN TO BE BOLD

PROBLEM: You Are Too Laid Back and Timid
RX: Speak Up for Your Rights—and for What's Right

"Fortune befriends the bold."
—John Dryden, 18th Century Author

Timid people may be likable. But on the job those *most* likable—from the boss's point of view in particular—are employees who step boldly up to make themselves heard and take over when their help is needed. Nobody likes a loudmouth. But if you are smart and tactful you can call favorable attention to yourself without being a loudmouth.

■ Speaking Up and Moving Up

Mr. Simon, who headed the Credit Department, slapped a hand to his forehead and groaned, "Oh no, not another fat report to prepare!"

The department head was overburdened with work, and took a briefcase full of work home most days of the week. No less overworked was his assistant John Gamboli, who planned on retiring before the end of the year, no matter what.

"I'd be glad to take over that report," piped up Barry, one of four hourly employees. Barry kept it no secret that he hoped to take over John's job once his resignation was official.

Mr. Simon frowned. "But you never—"

"—no problem, sir; I'm a fast learner."

Fast climber too. His boss didn't have to consider long whether to give the ambitious young man a shot at John's job. It was just the break Barry was looking for. The odds are good that he will be off the clock pretty soon.

KNOW WHEN TO WAVE THE RED FLAG

Boston-based management consultant Peter J. Lewis says, "No organization I know, manufacturing or service, public or commercial, is problem free and trouble free. Sharp observers, particularly if employed on a day-to-day basis by any enterprise you could name, are in a prime position to pinpoint headaches, hassles, and roadblocks. And I can tell you this from long experience. Every one singled out is an opportunity for the individual who is savvy enough to identify it."

> "The more problems . . . you can pinpoint and help solve or alleviate, . . . the quicker the top brass will come to know you are . . . a force to be reckoned with."

Industrialist Henry J. Kaiser referred to problems as "opportunities in work clothes." With this thought in mind it makes good sense to come to work "well dressed."

The more problems—hassles, roadblocks, safety hazards, bottom-line busters—you can pinpoint and help solve or alleviate, the more of a hero you will be and the quicker the top brass will come to know you are on the beam and a force to be reckoned with.

Are You an Opportunity Seeker?

Do you mine where the gold is the richest? Take the following short quiz to find out. Place a check mark alongside each item that rings a bell as it applies to your workplace, either within or outside of your own department or work area. When you are done, respond to the two questions that follow and rate yourself at the end.

(Note: If you do not own this copy of Job Smarts, *then be sure to make a photocopy of this quiz before you mark your answers.)*

	YES	NO
1. Can you point to any racism or other forms of bigotry in your organization?	——	——
2. Have you observed any incidents of sexual harassment?	——	——
3. Can you pinpoint any friction between employees in your area?	——	——
4. Do you know of any departments or work groups that fail to cooperate with each other?	——	——
5. Can you spot any bottlenecks that hold up the steady flow of work?	——	——
6. Can you cite any work procedures that are not as clear as they should be?	——	——
7. Do you know of any safety hazards that should be investigated?	——	——
8. Can you think of any work conditions or situations that could turn into a potential grievance?	——	——
9. Can you point out any work areas where employees need more training?	——	——
10. Can you cite any areas where plant or office security is weak?	——	——
11. If too many good employees are resigning, can you cite the reason why?	——	——

	YES	NO
12. Do you know of any supervisors who fail to give subordinates the credit and recognition they deserve?	___	___
13. Is it your belief that your organization finds it hard to hire good people because its wages and benefits are not competitive?	___	___
14. Have you run across any dishonest actions or trans-actions?	___	___
15. Do you know of any work problems you could help solve if you were given the chance?	___	___
16. Can you come up with an idea to make needed space available?	___	___
17. Can you suggest a way to make one of your company's products or services more competitive?	___	___
18. Can you figure out ways to reduce or eliminate waste of supplies or materials?	___	___
19. Can you come up with an idea to help alleviate your organization's parking problem?	___	___
20. Can you pinpoint any tools or equipment that are being discarded prematurely?	___	___
21. Can you spot any reasons why Competitor A or B seems to be more successful than your company?	___	___
22. Do you think you know why response to your organization's suggestion plan hasn't been as successful as it might have been?	___	___
23. Do you think your company's processing machines are producing too much scrap?	___	___
24. Do you have any ideas that might make it easier for your organization's workers with disabilities to per-form their jobs?	___	___
25. Can you figure out a way to combine two forms into one or three into two?	___	___

What's Your Opportunity Quotient (OQ)?

◆ With your workplace in mind, how many of the 25 items on the above list ring a bell?

◆ How many items can you add to the list?

◆ *Most importantly,* how many items can you think about creatively and come up with a suggestion for improvement?

It doesn't take an advanced degree to stand out from your workplace competitors who are shooting for the same career plums you are after. Enter 5 for each item you marked as an opportunity for improvement, then write your total score below.

Your Score _____

Now here's the good news: With a final score of no more than 15—a mere three items in your sights—you can be well on your way.

Opportunities for improvement pop up all over the place if you have the imagination and ambition to look for them. No one expects you to turn into a super-employee overnight. But all you need do is scroll down the preceding list for an idea of the multitude of potential problems, hassles, and better ways to do the job that exist in virtually every office, plant, warehouse, store, and showroom nationwide. Corruption, selfishness, and greed are only rarely involved. But where they are, finding a discreet way to expunge them will benefit everyone in the organization. Whatever the case, the preceding list—plus whatever items you can add—highlights the volume and diversity of situations that cause executive heads to gray prematurely. These are situations where good ideas and assistance will be more than welcome. Or put another way, these are *opportunities where judicious and thoughtful attention could make an ambitious young person stand out from the crowd.*

CLIMB ON THE CUSTOMER'S BANDWAGON

Here's good news!

In response to a consumer poll, two out of three customers say salespeople "just don't care." Retail and wholesale buyers are ringing up more complaints nationwide than ever before.

Qualtec Management Consultants, a firm that specializes in customer service management, states on its Web site that many organizations regard customers as a continuing source of irritation who disrupt their day to day operations.

New York-based marketing executive Valerie Kornblum estimates that the quality of customer service has fallen 15 to 20 percent in the past decade. She estimates that a 10 percent decrease in service has a more detrimental effect on corporate sales and profits than a 10 percent price increase.

The title of a *Reader's Digest* article asks bluntly: "Whatever Happened to Customer Service?" And two out of three consumers interviewed by the nationally known polling firm Yankelovich Partners believe that "salespeople don't care much about them or their needs."

So, hey come on! How is all of this *good news?* Quite simply. It represents an unprecedented opportunity for any savvy climber determined to jump start his or her career. The reason is clear. Anyone who has ever owned or run a business can confirm that if you take away a company's roster of loyal customers, all that remains is an empty shell. Employees who provide outstanding service can help ensure customer loyalty and are an employer's most valuable asset. Study after study of the nation's top-paid executives prove that the most powerful tool in a manager's arsenal is the ability to out-serve the competition and keep customers happy and loyal. As Valerie Kornblum states the case: "Call an outstanding customer service contribution to management's attention loud and clear and your name will not be forgotten."

■ Tim's Transformation

Today Tim is a full-fledged salesman earning $67,000 a year. Two years ago he was an impatient and frustrated young man. That's a tough combination to live with. Less than a year out of high school, he was one of seven members on the order board of a pharmaceuticals supply house in town. Soft spoken and shy, he finally woke up to the realization that unless he took *some kind of action,* he could be stuck in the rut of doing the same dull job five or even 10 years down the pike. A depressing situation.

Tim regularly reads a career column in the local paper. In one issue the column's lead paragraph set him thinking. "Laid back and timid? That is no way to grow and advance on the job," it read. The column went on to point out that to attract the favorable attention of the people who count in your organization, you have to blow your own horn, stand up and be heard. And there's no better way to stand up and be heard than by performing outstanding customer service.

> "There's no better way to stand up and be heard than by performing outstanding customer service."

Laid back and timid, that's me, Tim thought. But what could he do about it? Soon after this, however, Tim was struck by an idea that altered his life in general and his career path in particular. The customer's importance was always being stressed in his company. An article in the latest issue of the company magazine read, "Regardless of who your supervisor might be, your real boss is the customer. The customer is not only your boss, but *your* boss's boss as well, and *his* boss's boss. What the customer says goes. If enough customers desert the ship, it sinks. And everyone's job goes with them."

For a long time Tim had wondered about one customer in particular, Kelso Pharmaceuticals, a major employer in town. Kelso had never deserted Tim's company for the simple reason that it had never been a customer. Tim wondered why. Kelso was only 10 minutes away, yet it dealt with a supplier from another state. Mr. Griffin was the sales rep who handled the territory, and Tim asked him about the situation. The salesman had replied, "Young man, do you know what nepotism is?"

Tim wasn't sure. "No sir, I don't."

"Well, that's the problem. Nepotism means favoring a relative with the business. Kelso's purchasing agent is the brother-in-law of the district sales supervisor of the company it deals with. Kapische?"

Tim frowned. "Yeah, I guess so." But it didn't make sense.

Tim knew Mr. Thornton, the president and CEO of Kelso Pharmaceuticals. Well, he didn't exactly know him. Mr. Thornton played golf every Sunday, and when Tim was still in high school he used to caddy for him. Maybe this was his chance, once and for all, he thought, to stand up and be heard. He had nothing to lose.

That Sunday he went out to the golf course bright and early before Mr. Thornton approached the first hole. "Well, hello there, Tim. What are you doing here? Don't tell me you're still caddying?"

"No sir." Tim told him where he was working.

"Good for you. An excellent company."

"Yes sir, one of the best. And we're just a short distance away from your plant. If you dealt with us you would save on transportation. And when you run out of an item you need in a hurry, we could get it to you within minutes. I'm wondering why you aren't doing business with us."

The executive frowned. "That's a good question," he said. "Tell you what . . . "

He pulled out his wallet and gave Tim his business card. "Have your sales manager give me a call."

"Thank you, sir, I will."

You can fill in the rest of the story. Thanks to Tim, his company clinched the Kelso account. Tim was pulled off the order board and promoted to Sales Trainee. A few months later he was given a territory of his own, and today he's headed no place but up. And of one thing you can be sure: He is no longer laid back and timid.

Service, Service, Service

Exceptional customer service offers as good an opportunity as any to stand out and get yourself noticed. Here are a few field-based examples:

■ Paper Products Company

Tess was employed in the Billing Department. Customers frequently called to determine the stock status of particular items or check on past due deliveries. Tess went out of her way and then some in an effort to answer their questions and relieve their anxieties. She was so caring and helpful that many customers called her boss to express their appreciation. No one was surprised to learn that a few weeks ago Tess was promoted to assistant supervisor of the Customer Relations Department.

■ Department Store

John works in the Carpeting Department. In time, after an increasing number of shoppers asked specifically for John because he was the most knowledgeable, dependable, and helpful salesperson, management got the message. Today John is a senior associate in charge of customer service. His motto: Whatever the customer expects, give him a little bit more.

■ Liquor Wholesaler

Jeff was an assistant sales manager. It was the holiday season. One morning, after realizing he had not received an order from Max, a good customer, in some time, he gave Max a call. Max sounded upset. "I'm on my way to the hospital. Gert's scheduled for a hip replacement operation." Jeff expressed his sympathy and hopes for successful surgery and a speedy recovery. Then he asked, "Who's taking care of the store?" Max sighed and said, "No one; I'll have to close for the day." "No way!" Jeff snapped back. "It would cost you a bundle. I'll be right over." "But—" Max said, "No, I'll be there in 10 minutes." Jeff took over and did a thriving business for his friend and good customer that day and the next. Do you think Max could ever forget that and, no matter what, switch to another supplier? Do you think Jeff's good work and loyal friendship wasn't noticed by management? It works. Whatever the customer expects, give him a little bit more if you can.

> "Whatever the customer expects, give him a little bit more."

■ Auto Products Distributor

Grant, like Tim, is employed on an order board. Many customers who phone in ask for Grant when they have a particular question or problem. With his extensive product know-how, Grant suggests to callers the best product to fill a particular need—even if it means advising the customer to call a competitor to get the job done. No wonder Grant is now head of the order board and on his way up.

> "There's no better way to blow your own horn and get noticed than by dreaming up ways to improve customer service."

■ Cosmetics Manufacturer

Eileen, as a receptionist, is smart enough to realize you can't win an argument with a customer. Despite the pressure of her job, she never loses her cool and is always friendly and polite. No matter how unreasonable an angry, demanding customer might be, she usually comes up with an imaginative way to cool down a hot situation. The word gets around. So does Eileen—from one promotion to another.

So it goes. Have you been too timid and laid back for too long? There's no better way to blow your own horn and get noticed than by dreaming up ways to improve customer service. If experience holds true, the success of your innovations will bounce back to boost both your status and income.

Are You a Customer Service Pro?

Or, put another way, do you think like your company's CEO? Let's find out. Assuming that you have direct or indirect contact with customers on the job, the following quiz will help you rate yourself.

(Note: If you do not own this copy of Job Smarts, then be sure to make a photocopy of this quiz before you mark your answers.)

	YES	NO
1. Has the importance of superior service been drummed into your head?	___	___
2. Are you knowledgeable about your company's products?	___	___
3. Are you knowledgeable about your competitors' products?	___	___
4. When you're not sure of the answer to a customer's question, do you ever guess?	___	___
5. Are you a good listener?	___	___
6. Do you believe there's no such thing as a "problem customer"?	___	___
7. Do you have access to experts when you need help with a customer's problem or inquiry?	___	___
8. After helping a customer, do you ask for feedback to ensure satisfaction?	___	___
9. Do customers have to call more than once to resolve a problem or complaint?	___	___
10. Is it difficult for a customer to determine the status of an order that was placed?	___	___
11. Do you always return customer calls quickly?	___	___
12. In dealing with customers, are you alert to goodwill-building opportunities?	___	___
13. Do you regard a promise to a customer as sacred?	___	___
14. Are customer service standards well established and monitored at your workplace?	___	___
15. In conversations with customers do you try to keep a megasmile in your voice?	___	___
Your Score	___	___

■ **Rate Yourself.**

Score one point for every "yes" answer except to questions 4, 6, and 7 where a "no" answer gets the point. Assuming that this quiz is applicable to your personal dealings with customers, a perfect score is 15. Since it is the CUSTOMER who rules the corporate roost, anything less than perfection should gave you something to think about—and something to work on.

DON'T HANG BACK— ## CLAIM THE TREATMENT YOU DESERVE

"Well, I don't know, Beth. I sympathize with your problem, but I can't afford to jeopardize the department's structure and scheduling."

Beth's spirits sank several notches. Her boss, Bill Irwin's response to her request for flextime was a great disappointment. Beth liked her job as a tax manager in the accounting firm that employed her. The pay and fringe benefits were above average. She enjoyed the work and was darned good at it in the bargain. But if she had to choose between holding on to her job and keeping her child out of daycare, she felt staying at home with her two-year-old was the only choice she could make. But she felt having to make this choice wasn't fair.

She made that point to her boss. "My request is reasonable," she said. "Key employees in other departments are permitted to work nonstandard hours to accommodate family needs. Why not the tax department?"

"Every department has its own unique requirements," Mr. Irwin replied.

Beth wasn't satisfied with this answer, but she was reluctant to resign. Since her husband was going to school full time, she had become the family's sole source of financial support and couldn't afford to take chances. On the other hand, she didn't intend to sit still for her boss's callous rejection. Maybe she wouldn't have to resign after all. Beth brainstormed and devised a two-step plan.

Step one was to shop the market for a job she could fall back on if need be. As she suspected, she had no trouble landing one. The problem was that as a six-year employee, she would have to take a substantial cut in both status and salary, money she could scarcely afford. She didn't like having to do so, but tentatively accepted the lower paying job before proceeding with her plan.

Step two led her to Mr. Morris's office. Ted Morris was the company's financial vice president and Mr. Irwin's boss. Beth explained her predicament. "I like the firm and enjoy the work," she said. "I would hate to resign."

"And I would hate to lose you," Mr. Morris replied.

"Thank you. But I can't short-change my child. I know I can be just as productive putting in the hours I proposed on my request. I think it's unfair that I'm not given the chance."

The executive frowned. "Thanks for coming to me. I'll talk to Bill Irwin."

Mr. Morris talked to Mr. Irwin, and Mr. Irwin talked to Beth. Result: She is still employed with the firm under a schedule that is adjusted to her family's needs. And she is no less productive or hasn't lost income.

Moral of the story: Sometimes it pays to speak up. Especially when the alternative is unacceptable.

Management consultant Leonard J. Smith offers these feisty words of advice: "Don't *negotiate* when you are in a position to make demands." He adds, "That doesn't mean you should act like the indispensable resident genius without whom the company would go bankrupt tomorrow. But in a firm and tactful way, make it clear to the powers that be how badly they need you."

Fortunately Beth was well positioned to take Smith's advice. Look at your own situation and determine if you're in the same boat. As he points out, this is the year of the employee. If you have what it takes, a smart boss won't want another employer to take you away. So, if you are in a spot like Beth, it might be the right time to demand your just due.

■ Case in Point—Glen K.

A Chicago consulting group wanted very much to hire software specialist Glen K. Glen was willing to take the job, but he had one hiring condition: He and his wife wanted to start a family; however doctors had discovered that Glen had a low sperm count. The condition that Glen demanded of the consulting firm was that the company pay for expensive infertility treatments. The employer agreed.

■ Case in Point—Pauline S.

Pauline S., a law school graduate at the top of her class, had received no less than nine job offers. Her first preference by far was a firm within commuting distance of both her home and her fiancee who had been employed as an accountant nearby. She told the recruiter that she would love to work for his firm, but she would need to receive $5,000 more in annual salary. The recruiter hemmed and hawed, made a phone call, and eventually gave in.

■ Case in Point—Ed K.

Ed K., was an ace software programmer whose career goal at the moment was a systems management job. When Ed saw that his name had been excluded from a posted list of employees selected for advanced training he blew a fuse. Stomping up to his supervisor, he demanded, "Jim, why isn't my name on that list?" Jim nervously moistened his lips. "Sorry, Ed, it must have been an oversight."

Moral of these stories: Speak up to get what you want and need.

STICK OUT YOUR NECK WHEN YOU HAVE NOTHING TO LOSE

You're fed up with your job and being underpaid is just half of it. You aren't getting the assignments you like and feel you can do well. Your requests to be transferred to another department or division have been delayed or ignored. That promotion you've been promised hasn't come through. You don't get along with your supervisor. The training you anticipated has been postponed. Or, put another way, you are spinning your wheels, getting no place in a hurry, watching the world pass you by. So where do you go from here?

The quick and simple answer is to give notice and find another job or—always better when your decision is to walk—to find another job first, *then* resign.

But hold on a minute. You feel good opportunities with your present employer *would* exist, if only you could get transferred, promoted, assigned to another supervisor, signed up in that training program, or some other "if." Not to mention the advantages you might want to think about twice before giving up: your stake in the pension fund, the friends and contacts you made, the benefits your seniority yields, the income you may or may not be able to duplicate, the company's convenient location, and so forth.

Whatever advantages apply to you. The point is this. It is easy out of frustration, anger, or bitterness to give up what you've got and venture again into the Great Unknown without knowing what you may get. Of course, sometimes no choice exists. If you're in the wrong job or wrong organization, your smartest decision could well be to walk. But before closing the door, it might be a good idea to ask yourself: What about all those "if's"?

This is where your boldness and daring come into the picture. If you could only make one or more of the crucial *ifs* come to pass, it could delouse your job faster than weed killer spread on crabgrass. The first question to ask yourself is: Should you or shouldn't you stick your neck out and try to improve your current job situation? Which in turn triggers the second question you have to ask yourself: What do you have to lose?

Good questions. Florida *Sun-Sentinel* career specialist Lona O'Connor recommends finding yourself what she refers to as a "courage mentor" to help you answer them. "You probably haven't thought of courage as a career strategy," she writes and goes on to explain its crucial role. It takes courage to spring back from setbacks, to learn a hard discipline until you have mastered it, to stay focused on a tough assignment instead of saying "I can't do it."

It takes courage, too, to insist on what you deserve—to fight for that promotion, raise, transfer, or training opportunity—in the face of resistance. *And the time it makes the most sense to display such courage is* **when you have nothing to lose** *or*, put another way, when your current job situation is unacceptable.

But sometimes you need help. That's when a courage mentor can come to your rescue. Where can you find one? Almost any-where—at home, on the job, in your place of worship, or through social groups. The trick, says O'Connor, is "to identify some-one—a coworker, manager, friend, or family member" who is knowledgeable and sympathetic to your need. A savvy courage mentor will encourage you to fight for that promotion, raise, training, and so on because it is your due. And if you already decided that the status quo is unacceptable, then you have noth-ing to lose. So why not give risk a try? Why not stomp down your timidity and give it a shot?

■ Case In Point—Lisa

Lisa was ambitious. Her career goal, at least for the foreseeable future, was promotion from copywriter to account executive. But achieving that goal in the advertising agency where she had put in three hard years seemed as likely to her as being appointed a partner. The agency employed eight copywrit-ers. During the past year, two of them, both male—what else?—had been advanced to junior account exec, the first step, necessary in the process to become an account executive.

> "A savvy courage mentor will encourage you to fight for that promotion . . . because it is your due."

Lisa was mad enough to scream, which may have made her feel better momen-tarily, but she was too laid back and timid to open her mouth. She was clearly and undeniably the agency's most talented and over-worked copywriter, and if *anyone* deserved a promotion it was Lisa. When she meekly complained to John Hennessy, the partner in charge, he was sympathetic. "Lisa, you have a great future here. Be patient." She had been told that before. Her patience was running out.

Jerry Hirsch was one of the agency's top illustrators. He and Lisa had played racketball a couple of times after work, and he considered her a friend. One day Jerry noticed her scanning the help wanted ads. He invited her to lunch.

"Don't tell me you're thinking of leaving."

When she didn't reply, he added, "I don't blame you."

Lisa sighed. "Jerry, I've had it with this outfit. Hennessy stalled me on that promotion again."

Jerry nodded. "His 'be patient' routine?"

"What else?"

"So your response is to walk out."

"What choice do I have?"

"Maybe one—since there is no risk involved. Take my word for it, Lisa, Hennessy doesn't want to lose you. He'd be in a hole without you."

"He has some way of showing it," she snorted.

"Do me a favor," he said. "Your professional expertise is in demand in this market. Stomp into Hennessy's office. Don't bother to ask for an appointment. And lay your cards on the table. Either, or. You get the promotion, or you resign."

"You're crazy, Jer."

"You think so? I'll make you a bet: If you get the promotion, lunch at Four Seasons is on you; if you don't, it's on me."

Lisa took him up on the bet. She lost the bet. But more important, she won at the workplace with a promotion. As journalist Lona O'Connor points out and as Jerry proved, anyone can be a courage mentor.

FRONT AND CENTER
WHEN THE BOSS IS IN A BIND

So you are naturally laid back and timid. Not the volunteer type. No matter. The secret to newfound success is as close as the end of your arm. All it takes is a simple personality adjustment. In virtually every workplace with 20 or more employees on the payroll, troubles are always erupting. There are fires that need to be put out—production bottlenecks, irate customers, shipments that refuse to get shipped, breakdowns of one kind or another. The kind of emergencies that turn supervisory heads gray. Tough on the boss. A great opportunity for you. There is no better time to shine then when the boss is in a bind. If you want your supervisor to think kindly of you when merit increases or promotion decisions are being made, hang close by with those four magic words when crunch time is at hand:

How Can I Help?

Or better still, instead of *asking* how you can help, *tell* the boss how you can help. Spell it out in detail if need be. For a clue on how this can work, take a tip from Bill Berner.

■ Bill's Coming Out Party

Bill Berner was soft-spoken and shy. Not at all outgoing. He enjoyed working with his hands, anything mechanical, the more complex the better. His job description in the Maintenance Department at the plant was headed "Machine Shop Helper." Bill liked his job, but he would have liked it better if there were challenges. Two years ago, after he had graduated from high school, he attended vocational school and finished with a

Completion Certificate. Now he was biding his time, waiting for a more challenging opportunity to come his way.

Waiting.

Sometimes waiting isn't enough. A guy has to *do something* to make opportunity happen. Bill's best friend at the plant was Greg Schwartz. One day when the end-of-shift buzzer sounded Bill and Greg walked together on their way to the time clock to punch out. Bill asked, "What does Vince look so upset about?"

Vince was their foreman.

"He's got reason to be upset," Greg replied. "He may have to call off the second shift. Production is stalled. The big molding machine broke down. Bernie's on vacation, and Phil Belucci, the only other guy who can fix it, is out sick. Production is on Vince's back and the plant manager is blowing a fuse."

"I can fix that machine," Bill said.

"You can?"

"Sure. No problem."

"Hey, you wanna make a buddy for life . . . "

But Bill was already on his way back to the foreman's office. When Vince learned Bill could come to his rescue he greeted him like a long lost friend. And he never forgot it.

Moral of the story: Help your boss out when he or she is in a bind, and it could boost you a notch or two up the ladder. By now Bill is up several notches.

CHAPTER LESSONS

✓ Speak up and you will get noticed and move up.

✓ Identify problems or inefficiencies at your workplace, then figure out how to improve the situation. As a problem-solver on the job, you will prosper.

✓ The customer is the most important part of every business. Take care of the customer, and you will be sure to gain their appreciation as well as that of your boss. Then you can step up on the career ladder.

✓ When you are an in-demand employee, use your value to gain the schedule, pay, etc. that you need.

✓ If you aren't receiving the pay, other responsibilities, or other advantages that you believe you deserve and the situation is unacceptable, speak up. (Be sure to have a backup plan if your boss is unwilling or unable to meet your demands.)

✓ Find a courage mentor who will give you the confidence to fight for the raise or promotion that you deserve.

✓ Remember the four magic words: **How Can I Help?**

CHAPTER 6:
KNOW THE RIGHT PEOPLE

PROBLEM: You Don't Know the Right People
Rx: Find Yourself an Angel

> I have learned that getting a person to do what you want him
> to is simply a matter of leading his mind up four mental steps. First,
> you must get his favorable attention. Second, you must change that attention
> to real interest in the things you want him to do. Third, you must increase his
> interest until it becomes desire. Fourth, you must change that desire into action.
> —Clinton Davidson, Businessman and Author

"It's not *what* you know, it's *who* you know."

This may be one of the world's oldest clichés. But don't make the mistake of selling it short. Of course, from a career-building standpoint, *what* you know is of the utmost importance, as is made clear in chapter four, "The Knowledge Loop" and elsewhere in this book. But no matter how knowledgeable you become, if the message of what you know doesn't get through to the right people, your valuable savvy could be wasted.

WHO ARE THE RIGHT PEOPLE FOR YOU?

Let's say, for example, that you are an ambitious, young high school or college grad with career advancement in mind. Whose attention in your company should you try to attract to gain his or her favor? Should you set your sights on one or more of the elite? Or should your focus be broad? The quick answer might seem: attract the boss's favorable attention or *her* boss's attention, and you're on your way. That might sound good, but it is not always feasible. Too often, your boss, or her boss, will be too busy to notice you exist. It is far more practical to broaden your focus with the following three categories in mind: *The Boss Brigade, Your Coworkers,* and *Your Company's Customers.*

The Boss Brigade

No question about it. If you are in a position—or can maneuver yourself into a position—to do something imaginative and spectacular enough to make the brass sit up and take notice, it could be enough to jump start your career. But such opportunities don't pop up every day. What does occur on an ongoing basis is the opportunity to have the kind of job you do stand head and shoulders above the rest of the crowd. (The rest of the crowd being your coworkers who are competing for those wage boosts and promotions.) Remember that one of your boss's main responsibilities is to monitor his subordinates' performance. For one thing, this enables him to determine that departmental standards are upheld. For another, this allows her to decide who is in line for a wage increase or promotion. Finally, if your boss is savvy and is also ambitious, he keeps departmental succession in mind. For your boss to advance up the ladder himself, he will need to pick someone to step into his shoes when the time comes. So clearly, if you can come up with a brilliant idea that will make your boss shine or help him out of a tight spot, he is not apt to forget either your contribution or you.

> "If you can come up with a brilliant idea that will make your boss shine or help him out of a tight spot, he is not apt to forget either your contribution or you."

Your Coworkers

How well you get along with your associates and coworkers can make all the difference in how long it will take you to reach your career goals. Let's sit in on a meeting between Shipping Department Head Harry B. and his assistant Bruce to see how this works. The question at hand was whom to select as the leader of a new group that was being formed. The candidates under consideration have been narrowed down to three: Bert, Smitty, and Ruth.

Bert was smart, experienced, and had the most seniority. But Harry frowned when Bruce proposed his name. "He's a good worker," the supervisor observed, "but he has a short temper. That could make people resent him." "Yeah, that could be," his assistant conceded.

Choosing between Smitty and Ruth was tougher. Both were hard workers and personable. It was almost a toss-up, but not quite. Mulling over the records, Harry and Bruce agreed that Ruth, as the better team player, had an edge over Smitty. A number of incidents stood out. Ruth often went to bat for coworkers who were in a spot or was enthusiastic in response to a coworker's suggestion she found workable. More than once, Harry recalled, coworkers had expressed favorable comments about Ruth. No one would resent *her* promotion.

> "Cooperate willingly with your neighbors and teammates. In short, root for your coworkers' success and they will root for yours too."

As the old saying goes, "You scratch my back, I'll scratch yours"—by cooperating willingly with your neighbors and teammates you will be making a good impression on the right people. Pitch in with your help when it is needed. In short, root for your coworkers' success, and they will root for yours too.

Your Company's Customers

This asset was discussed in depth in the previous chapter. But bear in mind, customers are also the "right people" to know. Customers keep the corporate machinery moving. Never lose sight of the customer's influence on the powers that be. Get your customers rooting for you, and the message will get through to your boss.

Rate Yourself

How skillful are you persuading the *right people* in your organization to root for your success? Take the following quiz to find out. Answer the questions as honestly and objectively as possible. Then score yourself at the end.

(Note: If you do not own this copy of Job Smarts, *then be sure to make a photocopy of this quiz before you mark your answers.)*

	Often	Sometimes	Rarely
1. Do you show appreciation when someone helps you?	___	___	___
2. Do you become involved in the problems of others?	___	___	___
3. Do you encourage people to talk about themselves?	___	___	___
4. Do you wear a warm smile on your face?	___	___	___
5. Are you good at remembering peoples' names?	___	___	___
6. Are you a complainer?	___	___	___
7. Are you enthusiastic about the ideas of others?	___	___	___
8. Do you voluntarily pitch in when help is needed?	___	___	___
9. Do you go out of your way to get people to like you?	___	___	___

	Often	Sometimes	Rarely
10. Do you willingly share credit with coworkers?	——	——	——
11. Do you show respect for the opinions of others—even if you don't agree?	——	——	——
12. Do you admit it when you know you're in the wrong?	——	——	——
13. Are you influenced by personal prejudices?	——	——	——
14. Do you make good eye contact when listening?	——	——	——
15. Do you think people of the opposite sex are not as smart you?	——	——	——
16. Do you honestly try to see the other person's point of view?	——	——	——
17. Are you hot tempered?	——	——	——
18. Do you fight hard for an idea you believe in?	——	——	——
19. Do you support a friend's idea even if you think it's wrong?	——	——	——
20. Do you give praise where it's due?	——	——	——
21. When you are done with a job do you immediately seek another assignment?	——	——	——
22. Do you make personal sacrifices to help others?	——	——	——
23. On the job, do you view problems and bottlenecks as opportunities?	——	——	——
24. Are you too quick to criticize others?	——	——	——
25. Do you accept well-meant criticism in the spirit in which it is given?	——	——	——

Put Your Calculator to Work. For each question, circle the number that reflects your response. Then add all the numbers you entered to calculate your total score.

Question	Often	Sometimes	Rarely
1	5	3	0
2	5	3	0
3	5	3	0
4	5	3	0
5	5	3	0
6	0	3	5
7	5	3	0
8	5	3	0
9	5	3	0
10	5	3	0
11	5	3	0
12	5	3	0
13	0	3	5
14	5	3	0
15	0	0	5
16	5	3	0
17	0	3	5
18	5	3	0
19	0	0	5
20	5	3	0
21	5	3	0
22	5	3	0
23	5	3	0
24	0	3	5
25	5	3	0

Total Score   ____   ____   ____

How Do You Rate ? So, how successful are you at recruiting key people in your organization to your team? If your score is 125, you are either perfect (too good to believe) or, more than likely, deluding yourself. Any score above 100 is better than average and, as applies to every one of us, leaves some room for improvement. A score below 80 leaves plenty of room for improvement if you hope to have **the right people rooting for you.**

RECRUIT A WORKPLACE ANGEL

The playwright George Bernard Shaw once said, "In heaven an angel is nobody in particular." This doesn't apply in the workplace. In show biz—or on the job—the right angel can spell the difference between failure and success. On Broadway the right angel can keep the show running. If you work for Microsoft, and your angel is Bill Gates . . . well, you can finish this sentence yourself. The challenge, wherever you work, is to find your own special "Bill Gates." And if not the head honcho, then find someone as influential as possible.

> "On the job—the right angel can spell the difference between failure and success."

■ Ed Turner's Precipitous Rise

Ed Turner is an ambitious but underpaid, and underappreciated worker. He attends college in the evenings to earn his degree in business administration, and works during the day to help support himself and his family. You can't be much more ambitious than that.

One day his Management 101 prof advised the class to cultivate "angels" to help influence their growth on the job. "There are plenty of good jobs around," he explained. "But competition for the ripest plums and above average pay is tough and growing tougher. Getting a key executive to sponsor you can make your trip up the ladder faster and easier and more pleasant."

The prof's advice set Ed to thinking and brought Jason Blackwell, the company's Vice President of Marketing, to mind. Since Ed was in Data Processing he was well placed to be of use to Mr. Blackwell, and he made being useful one of his special priorities. Whenever the opportunity arose, Ed made it his business

to feed the executive timely information or make helpful suggestions to Mr. Blackwell. Before long, Mr. Blackwell started
calling on Ed for special data and reports. As he grew used to working with Ed and human nature being what it is, the VP became
interested in Ed and his goals and needs. It didn't take long for
the young man's customized attention to pay off—in spades and
in favors owed. His career path was shooting toward the stars. He
had acquired an angel.

With "angelic" thoughts in mind, take a tip from Ed's prof. On
a blank sheet of paper enter the names of potential prospects (key
players) in your organization who might appreciate your special
attention and help. Depending on where you are assigned, consider the following for one or more that might apply to your
work situation:

If You Are in the . . .

- **Sales Department:** Is there a way by which you can help an
  influential sales rep or customer service executive serve a
  customer more effectively? Do you have any ideas a sales manager might find useful with faster or more efficient service in
  mind? Are there any reports you can make more informative?
- **Billing Department:** Can you go out of your way if need be when
  the opportunity arises to give customers quick info in response
  to their inquiries regarding shipments or billing? Do this
  repeatedly and when the customer expresses appreciation, simply reply, "Thanks, but don't tell me, tell my boss."
- **Credit Department:** Credit is a perennial bugaboo and frequent
  source of customer irritation and resentment. Figure out clever

ways to help customers resolve credit disputes, and you will win brownie points that will add up in your favor.

- **Shipping Department:** When needed shipments are late, customers become edgy. Instead of regarding customer calls as annoying interruptions, try to make yourself the person customers ask for by name. Then make whatever effort you can to expedite delivery and/or soothe their anxieties. Your personalized concern will bounce back to your credit.

- **Customer Service Department:** Caring customer service workers—retail, wholesale, whatever—are more the exception than the rule in today's hectic marketplace. Make yourself the exception and you will stand out like a rose in a field of weeds.

Service sells faster than water in the desert. Wherever you work, whatever you do, make superior service your goal and—like the Golden Rule says: Do unto others as you would have them do to you. Caring service creates a positive boomerang effect rarely known to fail.

VOLUNTEER TO MAKE A DIFFERENCE

Don't read this wrong. For maximum effectiveness, your main motivation in volunteering for community service should be caring and compassion for people less fortunate than yourself. But at the same time, it can't hurt to keep this chapter's subject in mind: Getting to know the right people with career advancement as your goal. The rationale here is simple. If your voluntary efforts to ease the burden of people in need helps ease your own burden as well, as it invariably does, who is to fault the result or question your motive?

Have you ever thought about how participating in community service so often brings with it rewards to benefit one's career? Consider the following case histories.

■ Ernie K.

Ernie lived in the Bronx. His job as a sales clerk for a Manhattan food products distributor was as routine and dead end as you could imagine. Fortunately, Ernie was a good guy at heart. The pain and suffering of others touched him. The plight of poor city high school dropouts, in particular, distressed him. Without help, many of these kids would wind up on the street, or in jail or worse. Lacking job-based skills, the best they could hope for was to collect shopping carts at the supermarket or mop floors and wipe tables at the local fast-food emporium.

On his job Ernie had become a skilled computer operator. If those kids had some tech training, he reasoned, they might stand a chance. With this in mind, Ernie volunteered two evenings a week as an instructor at a community skills training program. What did he himself derive from this effort? Most importantly, he received personal satisfaction and gratification from working with kids who desperately needed his help. True, half of them dropped out of the program. But Ernie got to enjoy the feelings of success and accomplishment of the handful who stayed with the training and pulled themselves up as a result. This compensation was far greater than Ernie had ever experienced or expected.

> "Make a difference by selflessly serving others and the greatest difference you will make will be in the service you provide for yourself."
> —Ernestine Graf, Des Moines Sales Executive

On top of that, he received teaching experience he had no other way of getting. In time, when word of Ernie's newly developed skill and his contribution to the community reached the *right people* in management, he was transferred to his company's Training Department. Before long, a plaque on Ernie's desk read Training Supervisor.

■ Sally M.

"If you don't like the political system," Sally says, "instead of griping and grumbling, do something to change it." She believes, too, that one of the most important things any American can do is to register for his or her right to vote on Election Day. Disturbed by the poor showing in her neighborhood, Sally responded to an ad by her political party that solicited citizens to help Get Out the Vote. She was pleasantly surprised to find at the first meeting she attended that Mr. Givens, who headed the Advertising Department where Sally worked as a copywriter, was also involved in the Get Out the Vote effort. Mr. Givens quite definitely qualified as one of the "right people" in her company. And he was so impressed by Sally's imaginative ideas and enthusiastic cooperation at the meeting, that she automatically registered in his mind as a candidate for bigger and better things in the company.

■ Mildred C.

Mildred, who was employed as a sales correspondent in an insurance company near her home, felt that life had been good to her. She was healthy, had a good job, was happily married, and had a wonderful family. Feeling pay back time was at hand, she joined the local hospital's Volunteer Corps. Talk about coincidence! One day, Mr. Garcia, an executive in Mildred's company, was hospitalized. Imagine his surprise when, having rung for an attendant, who should appear but Mildred, wearing a pink volunteer's jacket. "What are *you* doing here?" he asked. "Oh, I volunteer four hours every Saturday," she replied.

It didn't take Mr. Garcia long to learn that Mildred's reputation for caring, compassionate service was second to none. Through her patience and sensitivity she helped make a difficult time as pleasant as possible, not only for him but for many other patients as well. One day, several weeks later, Mildred was summoned to a meeting with the head of the Human Resources Department and offered a nice promotion. Though she was delighted by the promotion, it came as a complete surprise to her. Why me, she wondered? She found out why the following day when Mr. Garcia, long recovered from his illness, called to congratulate her.

That's the way the rewards of volunteerism often work, sometimes when you least expect them. The joy and gratification of helping others are just one part of the benefits of volunteering. Rewards are sometimes felt in your paycheck as well.

■ Juan B.

Juan had immigrated to the United States as a teenager and worked hard to make his life better. Now 23, he had several accomplishments under his belt. He had learned English as a second language, earned his high school diploma, and became an inventory group leader at the textile company where he worked. Juan was headed up the company ladder, slowly, but surely.

Several other legal aliens worked in Juan's department and other departments in the company, but they mainly had low-paying jobs where English language skills weren't essential. It hurt Juan that these bright and conscientious people were stuck in dead-end jobs. If they could only speak English more adequately, they would have more opportunities. Juan decided to do something about it. He informed a selected handful of men and women with good potential that he would be willing to help them to improve their English skills at no cost to them. Before long he was conducting a class composed of eight eager students. Two dropped out. The progress of those who stayed was outstanding.

The word inevitably spread. To make a long story short, his company established a Department of Diversity Management. Who do you think was appointed its manager?

Any number of such stories can be told. The conclusion of each is that selfless volunteerism is often self-serving as well. Aside from the joy and gratification of helping others, how can you benefit from such service? South Florida marketing executive and author Robert E. Levinson cites the following benefits.

Volunteerism can . . .
- ◆ enhance your reputation as a kind and caring person
- ◆ advance your professional credibility
- ◆ develop and sharpen your management skills
- ◆ establish valuable contacts within your community
- ◆ win you "brownie points" on the job
- ◆ help you develop leadership skills
- ◆ familiarize you with educational programs
- ◆ provide experience attending meetings and conferences
- ◆ help you to make a difference and come out of your shell

How and Where Can You Help?

The need for volunteer help within the community can not be overstated. The ideal place to pitch in is where you feel you might be the most useful, and where you feel your involvement would give you the most gratification. Pick the kind of community program or cause that motivates you the most, then check it out. Here is a sampling of organizations and causes that may interest you.

Community Chest	Political Involvement
March of Dimes	Equal Rights—Women
Red Cross	Equal Rights—Minorities
Salvation Army	Computer Training
Disaster Relief	Language Training
United Way	Help for the Disabled
Big Bothers and Sisters	AIDS/HIV services
Shriners Hospitals	Help for the Elderly
Human Centers	Heart, Cancer, MS Fund
Homeless Helpline	Help for the Blind

To be assured of informed involvement, check your local library, or public information sites on the World Wide Web. Use the Web to search for groups in your area by typing in the keyword "Volunteering" and the name of your city.

WHAT STEPS CAN YOU TAKE TO ATTRACT MR. OR MS. RIGHT?

What would you do if you were the principal player in the following field-based situations? Make your personal decision before reading what actually happened.

■ Situation A: Mel

Mel had a BS degree, had worked for his company two years, and was eager to be assigned to the company's lab in rubber products. He was bright, personable, well liked, and had plenty going for him. But so did at least six associates, each no less ambitious than Mel. But he had an idea that, if it worked, might give him an edge over the competition. He thought Mr. Adams, an influential VP, was just the guy who could put in a good word for him. The executive did not know Mel any better than he knew the other candidates. But Mel's wife, Janice, knew *him*. She was a member of the church choir that Mr. Adams directed. In fact, Janice was a favored soloist.

Their relationship, Mel reasoned, might be used for him to become acquainted with Mr. Adams. Perhaps if Janice invited Mr. Adams to dinner some evening . . . His wife resisted the idea, feeling that Mel's motivation would be too obvious.

Question: In Mel's shoes would you press your spouse to make the dinner invitation?

What Happened: Janice finally gave in and extended an invitation to Mr. Adams and his wife. They thoroughly enjoyed the evening. The executive hadn't known Janice's husband was employed by his company. For his part, Mel was tastefully subtle and discreet and not in any way pushy. He hoped that the executive would take a personal interest in him but left any next step up to Mr. Adams. That's exactly what happened. The executive wanted to know all about Mel's job and what he did for the company. In time he recommended Mel for a transfer to the lab job he had been shooting for.

■ Situation B: Cliff

Junior auditor Cliff was no less ambitious than Mel. But like Mel, he needed help from Mr. Right. In Cliff's case, Mr. Right was Cal Raines, the company's financial vice president. The young auditor racked his brain. How could he get Mr. Raines to notice him? Cliff had an idea he thought might be worth a shot. The vice president was an avid golfer and a member of the town's most exclusive—and expensive—golf club. Cliff's dad was also a member. When Cliff golfed, he frequented the more affordable public links. But if he could persuade his Dad to take him to the club as a guest, it would give him a chance to approach Mr. Raines on an equal footing. He had nothing to lose. Or so he thought.

Question: How do you like Cliff's bright idea?

What Happened: Cliff had no trouble persuading his dad to take him to the club as a guest. After playing the course, he approached Mr. Raines who was sipping a drink at the clubhouse, dubbed the "19th Hole." "Hey there Cliff, what are you doing here? I didn't know you caddied." "I don't, Mr. Raines. I'm here as a guest of my dad who's a member. I just played 18 holes." "Oh, I see," he said. They chatted some more and Cliff steered the conversation around to his interests on the job. At that point the executive turned decidedly cool. "Son, I don't discuss business away from the office."

When Cliff told his father what he had done, his dad was embarrassed. "Cliff, your intentions were too obvious. If you want to attract Ed Raines's interest, you'll have to find some other way. Or better still, come up with a bright idea to improve the company's bottom line. That's a sure way to get management to notice you."

■ Situation C: Ellen

Ellen was employed as a word processing operator in an office equipment manufacturing company. She had a natural talent for systems and procedures, but she lacked the training and experience to win a transfer to the Systems Department. She had applied for admission to an advanced training program but hadn't been accepted, and she wasn't likely to be. Unless . . . unless she could come up with a brainstorm that would let the top brass know she was alive.

One day Ellen overheard a conversation between Mr. Perry, her supervisor, and Ms. Bernhart, the company's data processing vice president. They were expecting a big shipment of supplies and had no place to store them. "The warehouse," Mr. Perry said, "is more crowded than Times Square on New Years Eve."

The comment called to mind a recent conversation Ellen had with her friend Jane. Jane's company, which was nearby, had just discontinued a major product line. Since the company had done that, Ellen reasoned, they might have warehouse space to spare. Maybe they would rent some to a neighbor. Feeling she had nothing to lose, Ellen made a phone call to her friend. "Sounds like a good idea," Jane replied. "I'll check." Jane called her back within minutes. "My boss said he'd be happy to rent your company some space, as much as you need." "I'll get back to you," Ellen said.

Question: Does Ellen sound like a smart lady or Miss Buttinsky?

What Happened: You probably guessed the conclusion. Ms. Bernhart and Jane's boss made a mutually profitable deal before the day was over. And there's not a person in the executive suite who doesn't know how it happened or who set the idea into motion.

Want to make a hit with Mr. Right? Take a tip from Mel or Ellen, not Cliff. You can push for your own interests but do it tactfully.

CASH IN ON THOSE TWO MAGIC WORDS: "NO PROBLEM!"

From the boss's point of view, from *the boss's* boss's point of view, and from the CEOs point of view, no sweeter words were ever uttered when hassles and bottlenecks occur. To make Mr. or

Ms. Right think well of you, here are some made-to-order times to respond, **"No problem!"**

◆ When your supervisor asks you to work through your lunch hour and take lunch later because a rush order is behind schedule.

◆ When the boss asks you to change your vacation schedule because you can't be spared at the time you had planned to take.

◆ When you are asked to take on an additional assignment or project.

◆ Any time you are asked to pitch in.

◆ When asked: "Is this job too tough for you to handle?"

Get the message? It's a surefire key to success: Think of the boss's problem as *your* problem. When he or she is in need of your help, respond "No problem!" Mr. and Ms. Right will get the message.

■ Making It In Sales

Ted worked as a sales clerk in the wholesale liquor industry. Executives' income was known to be high in this field. Close on their heels as top earners were members of the sales force. The more lucrative the sales territory, the higher the salesperson's income was likely to be. Small wonder that one of the most sought after jobs was sales representative. Small wonder, too, that Ted, who attended college four evenings a week, had registered for as many sales and marketing courses as possible. He wanted to get into Sales Training so much he could taste it.

> "Think of the boss's problem as *your* problem."

Ted was bright and ambitious and a **No Problem** kind of guy. The company's biggest account was Central Liquor on Main. It was Friday evening, two weeks before Christmas, and the quitting buzzer had just sounded. Ted was about to head for the time clock to punch out when the telephone rang. Others ignored the ring. Not Ted. He figured the call might be something important, so he picked up the phone.

Mr. Molinari from Central Liquor was upset. He had suddenly discovered they were out of stock on Four Roses, one of the retailer's best-selling items. Liquor stores do 10 times their normal business during the weeks before Christmas and New Year's Eve. Being out of stock of a popular item on a weekend at this time of the year could cost the dealer a bundle in lost income.

Ted felt for the customer. "Let me if see anyone is still here," he said. "I'll get right back to you."

He made a beeline to Shipping. The dispatcher was just closing up. Ted explained the situation. "The drivers are all gone," the dispatcher told Ted. "The trucks are locked up."

"Give me a hand," Ted replied. "We'll load a dozen cases into the back of my car. I'll run them up there myself." The store was miles out of his way but he didn't give that a thought.

The dispatcher was glad to oblige. Ted telephoned Mr. Molinari and told him he was on his way. The customer couldn't have been more grateful.

"No problem," Ted replied. "I won't forget this," the retailer said.

He didn't. Word of such service gets around. Monday morning Mr. Molinari called Harry Rosen, the account representative. "That kid went out of his way and saved me a pile of dough. That's what I call service with a capital 'S'. He ought to be commended for it." "He will be," Harry promised. The rep called John Hamilton, his sales manager and passed the word up the line. "John, next time a Sales Trainee spot opens up—"

"Thanks, Harry, I'll keep it in mind."

That was two years ago. Today Ted covers his own territory as a rep. Any wonder?

A DIRECT LINE TO MR. OR MS. RIGHT

In almost any company you can name, the fastest and most direct line to Mr. or Ms. Right starts at the bottom—the bottom line, that is. Dream up ideas that improve your company's profitability and a warm place in management's heart will be assured. Check the following for a sampling of real-life examples.

■ Chemical Company

Garvin K. came up with an idea. He suggested replacing only the worn right or left work glove instead of the whole pair. This saved his company an estimated $2,200 a year and won him 10 percent of these savings. In addition to that, Garvin won a special vacation award for himself and his wife because he submitted the greatest number of accepted entries to the company's Suggestion System during the past year. That's not all he won. As a reward for his creativity and initiative, Garvin was promoted to a prime spot in the Systems Department.

■ Paperboard Manufacturer

Sally M. is creatively nosey. Snooping through the scrap barrel, she couldn't believe that so many units condemned as "overage" were beyond salvage and repair. All some of them needed, she felt, was the replacement of gaskets, seals, and other minor components. She brought this to the attention of her boss, the production supervisor, who launched an investigation. Long story made short, the company ended up having a $12,500 bottom-line return. This earned for Sally not only a suggestion award, but a letter of commendation from the company's general manager. You can bet that Sally is now on management's promotability list.

■ Publishing Company

Carlos P. was angry and ready to take action. After auditing his home telephone personal bill for the past year, he felt he was being ripped off by phone company errors for calls he never made and other excessive charges. It took him frustrating hours to get his billing straightened out, an ordeal that had been shared by more than one of his neighbors.

Carlos wondered, if his home billing was so full of mistakes, what must his company's billing be like? He started a little snooping on his own and found his conclusion confirmed. Carlos submitted a suggestion to management to have the company's billing audited by one of the companies that does such work on a shared saving basis. The result of this suggestion was an estimated annual cost reduction of more than $73,000.

> "Dream up ideas to boost your employer's bottom line and the chances are good that your own bottom line will be jacked up as well."

Was Carlos noticed by Mr. or Ms. Right? You can bet your bottom-line dollar on that.

Get the message? Dream up ideas to boost your employer's bottom line and the chances are good that your bottom line will be jacked up as well.

Successful business is a two-way street: Employer and employee working together to keep stockholders and customers happy. Just as you hunt for Mr. or Ms. Right with a career boost in mind, management is on the alert for promotable candidates qualified to meet tough challenges. If that shoe fits your foot, you could do no bigger favor for both management and yourself than to use the most powerful career-building tool in the book. Come up with *money saving and money making ideas* to call Mr. or Ms. Right's attention to your teamwork and initiative abilities—and your promotability.

CHAPTER LESSONS

✓ There are three types of people that will help you build your career: **Bosses, Coworkers,** and **Customers.**

✓ Cultivate an angel at work to help you move up on the job.

✓ Volunteer in your community, primarily because you care about people but also as a way to develop leadership and management skills, make contacts in the community, and get noticed by people that can help you in your career.

✓ Take steps to attract the attention of Mr. or Ms. Right so you can promote your own interests. *But* remember to be tactful

✓ Apply the following two words to your job: **No Problem**

✓ Treat your boss's problems as your problems.

✓ Ideas that save and make money for your company will win the heart of your manager and demonstrate your promotability.

CHAPTER 7: GET YOUR BOSS IN YOUR CORNER

PROBLEM: Your Boss Is Working Against You
Rx: Get the Boss on Your Team or Get Out

> **"The most important aspect of
> teamwork is getting the boss on your team."**
> —Richard R. Conarroe, Public Relations Executive

Craig's boss sported a crew cut. Craig wore his hair long. What does that have to do with holding Craig back on the job? Unfortunately, a great deal. The sad reality is that Craig's boss is as right-wing conservative as Craig is left-wing liberal.

Craig is bright and ambitious. But his ultraconservative boss could hardly care less. One day Craig groused to an associate about being bypassed for the promotion he was sure he deserved.

"Smarten up," his friend advised. "It's obvious. The big muck-amuck doesn't like your politics or the way you cut your hair. He doesn't like you, period."

"You mean . . . he's a bigot?"

His friend shrugged. "You said it, I didn't."

Life in the marketplace isn't always fair. Whether you're an executive, manager, or rank-and-filer, no one is more important to your income—and outcome—than your direct supervisor. If, for whatever reason, your supervisor isn't on your team, your best bet is to win him or her over if you can, or start checking the job market.

YOU'RE IN BAD WITH YOUR
BOSS: IS IT HIS FAULT OR YOURS?

■ Dan's Attitude

Dan K., who had been employed for seven months on the shipping platform of an office products distributor, didn't know what he hated more—his job or his boss. One thing was certain: No love was lost between the two men. Dan clearly wasn't one of Foreman Ed Metcalf's favorites. When it came to special training programs or preferred assignments, Mr. Metcalf didn't seem to know Dan existed. Although his job was boring, mostly hustling cartons and cases, Dan hadn't minded it at first, because the pay was above average and he felt there was a chance for advancement. In fact, his pal Gary, who had recommended him for the job, had been promoted twice since being hired a year before. Not Dan. He was spinning his wheels. Dan had been debating with himself for weeks now: Should he continue to fish or cut bait?

When Dan had been transferred to the regular payroll after passing his 30-day probationary period, his performance rating had been "Better Than Average." His next rating, two months later, had been downgraded to "Satisfactory." The one after that had slipped to "Marginal." Dan wasn't surprised. Who cares? he thought. He didn't have a future working under Mr. Metcalf. Mr. Metcalf wasn't doing anything for *him;* why should he break his butt for Metcalf.

Get the picture? Of course, the one question Dan might have asked was: *Why* hadn't he gotten a break? The answer early on could have been that perhaps there were no breaks available at that time. After all, he had only been there a short while. After the first few months, however, why had it never occurred to him that, with his performance sliding downhill, he might have disqualified himself for the break he was so sure he deserved? What supervisor in his right mind is going to advance an employee whose performance isn't up to standard? As the old saying goes, "What goes around comes around."

The Get Even Syndrome

Once your attitude pits you against your boss, your career will be doomed from that point on. Bosses have attitudes, too, and react accordingly. One supervisor I know was asked: "How many people work for you?" His reply: "About half." How do you think he feels about the other half?

In my many years as a manager, as a supervisor, and—most of all—as a grunt on the line, I must have heard Dan's rationale expressed 10,000 times: **"I'm getting a lousy deal from my boss, why should I knock myself out for him?"**

Because you don't knock yourself out for *your boss*, my friend—you knock yourself out for you. While it's true that the "Get Even" response to real or imagined unfair treatment makes it hard on the boss, the one it hurts most of all is the person who thinks he or she is getting even. This fact of life in the marketplace is so obvious it's surprising that Dan didn't trip over it. Untold thousands of young people in low-level jobs are stuck in ruts because they don't see the values of putting out their best effort. The point is that unless you put out your best effort you're destined to remain in a rut.

> "The point is that unless you put out your best effort you're destined to remain in a rut."

Why is Dan underpaid and stuck on a low rung of the career ladder, and what can he do about it? He has two simple options:

1. He can shift into reverse on the job and surprise the boss with his best possible performance. The odds are high that his turnaround will catch the boss's attention and that he will react in his favor. If he doesn't, option number two is still available.
2. Dan can throw in the towel, find another job, and start from scratch by changing his attitude and turning over a new leaf elsewhere.

YOU'RE GOOD AND YOU KNOW IT

Laura G., a young, bright, creative, and ambitious woman , got along fine as an assistant to Mona K., the owner of a small public relations agency. Laura loved her job. In her three years with the firm she had received steady promotions and wage increases. But life without problems would be dull. When Mona, age 60, decided to step down and put her daughter Gert in charge of the business, it turned Laura's career topsy turvy. She had never gotten along well with Gert. But prior to her boss's announced retirement, they hadn't had much to do with each other.

Now that Gert was at the helm, however, she had a great deal to say. Laura's status as an assistant seemed to be dissolving grain by grain. Laura was an extremely well-organized person; Gert was forgetful and disorderly. When Laura tried to set things straight, Gert's response was, "Don't worry, it will work out." But Laura found herself putting in hours of overtime in an effort to make things "work out." Laura believed in talking it over when misunderstandings occurred. Gert resorted to memos that were formal, condescending, and at times almost insulting. Laura was starting to doubt her own competence.

One day, in desperation, she appealed to Mona, who by now was putting in less than two days a week. Her ex-boss appeared to be sympathetic but was too distracted to take Laura's problem seriously. She echoed her daughter's sentiments. "Don't be so sensitive. Everything will work out."

But it didn't work out. One evening at home Laura broke into tears. She confessed all to her husband, Tim, a young up-and-coming middle manager. He listened thoughtfully, then said, "Let's sit down at the word processor." They did, and with Tim's help and guidance, Laura brought her resume up to date. As they did so, listing qualification by qualification Laura felt her self-confidence return. Within weeks she was happily employed elsewhere.

> "When you know you are good, and you're not treated right, sometimes flying the coop is the only solution."

When you know you are good and you're not being treated well, sometimes flying the coop is the only solution.

■ Underpaid and Unappreciated

The boredom was bad enough, but being ignored was worse.

Mark was the best junior auditor in the Accounting Department—the best of 14. The trouble was no one seemed to know it but Mark. Mr. Slocum, the chief auditor and Mark's boss, seemed to be the least aware of his abilities. Mark believed that he was more than well qualified for promotion to senior auditor. But most of the assignments Mr. Slocum gave him were child's play for even the greenest junior. Mark was bored and unchallenged. Nonetheless, he put conscientious effort into every job assigned and turned in perfect performance. Still, he kept getting more of what he regarded as "kid stuff."

Mark was ambitious. He was also smart enough to know that to develop, grow, and advance, a person has to build his knowledge and experience on the job. One of his professors in college had repeatedly impressed on the class: "If you don't learn on the job, you're kaput!" But because Mark was given simple assignments repeatedly, he had no chance to learn anything new and certainly no chance to advance.

On the other hand, he reasoned, his 10 months on the job wasn't that long. The grunt work had to be done and even though he felt himself to be levels above grunt status, he was reluctant to come across as dissatisfied and uncooperative. It was important to function as a member of the team. So, what to do? Mark was squeezed between the proverbial rock and a hard place. He might have turned to Arthur Simpson for guidance. Simpson is an auto industry executive who was credited with the saying: "Dissatisfaction is the first step toward progress."

That Mark was dissatisfied with his simple, nonproductive job assignments was a "get-ahead response." That he refrained from taking action on his dissatisfaction was a "stay-behind response." The point is that Mark had *nothing to lose* from going to his boss and . . .

◆ calling his attention to his advanced knowledge and savvy, and
◆ requesting more challenging assignments.

The odds are high that the chief auditor would have been impressed by Mark's initiative. Bosses categorically welcome subordinates who are willing and able to take on difficult tasks. With 14 auditors on his staff, it's a good bet that during his busy work day, Mr. Slocum had overlooked the young man's capabilities.

Moral of the story: Ignore a "get-ahead" response and you will get left behind.

That Bad Old "Good Old Boys' Club"

You're good and you know it. But if you are on the outside looking in, your knowledge may not do you much good. In corporate America the "Good Old Boys' Club" can be a very private organization. You could be denied admission for any number of reasons. Bluntly stated, some of the more obvious reasons for not being part of the "in" crowd are:

◆ You committed the unpardonable sin of being a woman. (Or, less commonly, a man).

◆ You're an old guy among young people. Or a young guy among more mature coworkers.

◆ The color of your skin doesn't blend well with that of Club members.

◆ You are an immigrant.

◆ You committed the unpardonable sin of being Jewish, Roman Catholic, or Muslim, or whatever the Club is not.

◆ You are a liberal among conservatives, a conservative among liberals, or in some way *different* from the Club's membership.

■ Family Circle

Often the surest way to be excluded from the private Club is simply being outside of the Family Circle, as Archie V. found out the hard way. Archie worked as a computer programmer at a brokerage firm, and it was generally known in the Systems Department that if the project was more demanding than usual, the guy to see was Archie. Regarded as something of a wiz, Archie was accorded the admiration and respect that were his due. In fact, he was accorded everything but the promotion to a higher level position that his competence and conscientious performance demonstrated he deserved. The reason? You guessed it.

The "Old Boy's Club" in the Systems Department was composed of the CEO's son and daughter, a nephew, and a niece. Only one other programmer and Archie were not family members. When higher level opportunities opened up, who do you think was promoted? Archie finally made the move he should have made months ago. He decided that coping with the Family Circle was too much for him, and he flew the coop. "There are some things about the old job I miss," Archie confesses. "But I sure don't miss the family."

No matter how knowledgeable you consider yourself, sometimes knowing when it is time to get out can be the most important know-how of all.

FACING UP TO REALITIES

On a scale of 1 to 10—1 representing love and 10 hate—how do you feel about your boss? Assistant Buyer Molly G., if asked this question, would promptly reply, "12!" If you ask Molly *why* she hates her boss, she could go on for hours. If you ask her why she doesn't quit, she would probably frown, moisten her lips, and remain silent, too embarrassed to speak. Molly's problem is twofold: For one thing, she needs the job; for another, she's an insecure person unable to take a risk.

What About You?

Do you hate your boss? If so, is it a generic feeling based on vague resentment and not specifically addressed circumstances? Or have you analyzed why you hate your boss? Maybe this is the time. Make an honestly objective evaluation of your feelings and the situation to determine if it would be in your best interest to resign, hang in there, or take some remedial action that might remedy the circumstances. Whatever your answer, this is as good a time as any to evaluate—or re-evaluate—your work environment. Assuming that you don't get along as well as you would like to with your boss, respond to the following quiz as objectively as you can. Then based on your total number of "yes" and "no" answers, decide if some kind of action is indicated.

(Note: If you do not own this copy of Job Smarts, *then be sure to make a photocopy of this quiz before you mark your answers.)*

		YES	NO
1.	Does your boss claim credit for your good ideas?	___	___
2.	Does your boss fail to give you the information you need to do a good job?	___	___
3.	Does your boss bypass you for deserved merit raises?	___	___
4.	Would you be astonished if your boss complimented you?	___	___
5.	Does your boss make promises and then break them?	___	___
6.	Would you evaluate your boss's work performance as incompetent?	___	___
7.	Do you feel your boss is a bigot?	___	___

	YES	NO
8. Do you think your boss is dishonest?	——	——
9. Does your boss commit sexual improprieties?	——	——
10. Does your boss fail to give you the training you need?	——	——
11. Does your boss play favorites in the work he or she assigns?	——	——
12. Is your boss part of an "Old Boys' Club" that excludes you?	——	——
13. Are your boss's politics opposite from yours and does he or she make that known?	——	——
14. Does your boss criticize you unfairly?	——	——
15. Does your boss ever embarrass you in front of others?	——	——
16. Does your boss yell at you?	——	——
17. Do you feel that your boss doesn't care about your personal well being?	——	——
18. Does your boss rarely, if ever, have time to listen to your problems or needs?	——	——
19. Is your boss a know-it-all, and doesn't listen to others' ideas?	——	——
20. Would your boss hurt others if he thought it would do him some good?	——	——
Total Number of YES and NO Answers	——	——

The "Yeas" Have It

How do you feel about your boss? Do you hate him passionately? Do you detest him intensely? Or do you simply feel a mild dislike? It's all in the numbers. Tally your "yes" and "no" answers above. If you checked 15 or more "yes" blanks, it's time for you to seek greener, and less toxic, pastures. Ten to 14 "yes" checkmarks should give you ample cause for reflection, six to nine should put you knee deep in a quandary. Any number under five should make you reflect that maybe part of the problem is you.

Does Your Boss Hate You?

If you answer "yes" to that question, the next key question is "Why?" Could your boss's antagonism be justified? Bosses are human, just like you and me, and have human needs and priorities. One of these is to get the job done. Are you part of the problem or part of the solution? Have you given your boss cause to be prejudiced against you? Or is he or she just a mean and hateful person? Let's find out. The more honest and objective your responses to the following questions are, the more useful your self-evaluation will be.

	YES	NO
1. When your boss is in a spot do you feel it's not your concern?	——	——
2. Do you goof-off too often?	——	——
3. Are you a chronic absentee?	——	——
4. Are you often late for work?	——	——
5. Do you extend lunch or break periods?	——	——
6. Do you give the boss a hard time when asked to work overtime?	——	——
7. Do you bad-mouth the company, its products, or leaders?	——	——
8. Are you too often resistant to change?	——	——
9. Do you regard a job's completion as an automatic rest period?	——	——
10. Do you feel teamwork doesn't apply to you?	——	——
11. Are you away from your work station too often?	——	——
12. Do you often argue with coworkers?	——	——
13. Do you ever get into hassles with customers?	——	——
14. Are you a chronic complainer?	——	——

	YES	NO
15. Do you take constructive criticism personally?	___	___
16. Are you reluctant to share information with coworkers?	___	___
17. Do you often guess when you don't know the answer?	___	___
18. Does your performance have to be closely monitored?		
19. Do you abuse email privileges?	___	___
20. Do you engage in long personal telephone conversations?	___	___
Total Number of YES and NO Answers	___	___

The Nays Have It.

In this quiz the naysayers are the good guys. Every "yes" answer earns you a "J"—"J" for "Justifiable." The more "Js" you tally, the greater your boss's justification is for feeling antagonistic and for working against you. If you tallied 10 to 14 "Js" ("yes" answers) your career may be on thin ice; if you have 15 or more it's no wonder your boss can't stand the sight of you.

How does your boss feel about you? Do you feel excluded from his list of favorites? Do you believe he's indifferent to you and your needs? Does he dislike you? Or does he out and out *hate* you? Is your boss *J-Driven?* Are his true feelings governed by the number of "Js" ("yes's") you scored on this quiz? Generally speaking, the easier you make the boss's job, the more kindly disposed he will be towards you. As an employee interested in career growth and advancement, the less "Js" you score, the better your chances will be to win the boss's friendship and support. (*If you tallied a relatively small number of "Js," and your boss is still working against you, it may be time to either acquire a new boss or a new job.*)

KNOW THY BOSS

Do you know what you want from your life and career? Do you know what your boss wants from his or her life and career? Do you understand the role your boss plays in meeting your goals? Do you understand the role you play in meeting your boss's goals?

"Know thyself," Socrates counseled. Experience proves that from a career standpoint it is just as important to "know thy boss." No reality of the marketplace could be simpler or clearer. No one is more important to your career success than your direct supervisor. Yet, despite this reality, it's amazing how many millions of job-holders act as if the boss is their worst enemy.

You don't have to get an "A" in Psychology 101 to realize that if you expect people to respond to *your* needs, you have to respond to *theirs.* All you need to do is bring to mind the Golden Rule. It is human nature for the boss to do unto you what you do unto the boss. Before doing unto others, though, you need to know what others want to have done. It is at best awk-

> "No one is more important to your career success than your direct supervisor."

ward and at worst career-ending, to deal with your boss day after day without understanding his or her needs, aspirations, and goals. With this thought in mind, take a tip from Anne K.

■ One More Time: "One Hand Washes the Other"

This old saying is worth repeating again and again. At least that's what new car sales rep Anne K. believed. Anne was as ambitious as she was hardworking, conscientious, and bright. She was also smart enough to know that for a person to succeed at any job, in addition to being qualified, she must also get on the good side of her boss and get her boss rooting for her. Focusing on this goal, Anne placed Alex Johns, her sales manager, under a high powered microscope. "The trick," she said, "is to keep the boss's business goals in view at all times and help achieve them if you can."

> "Success is a matter of luck— ask any failure." —Anonymous

She gave this example. A goal common to many dealerships is to generate so many sales that their manager earns the special manufacturer's bonus offered for surpassing the monthly sales quota. This isn't always easy to do. Automakers aren't charitable organizations. Tough quotas are set, which is why generous bonuses are offered for reaching them. A few months ago, Anne noted that her dealership was a shade short of reaching its quota.

Anne had a talk with her boss. "Alex, just how close are we?"

Notice her use of the word "we." It's a powerful word. *We! Us*—you and me as a team. The message is clear. Anne wanted her boss to know that his earnings goals were her goals as well.

Alex mentioned a figure. "Wow, we're almost there," Anne replied.

"Yeah," he answered gloomily, "but you know the old saying: A miss is as good as a mile. It's already the 22nd of the month. That doesn't give us much time."

Anne gritted her teeth. "We can do it," she said.

Her statement was more than moral support. She proposed giving the car shoppers she served between now and the end of the month a special discount to induce them to buy. "Hopefully, that should boost sales over the edge."

"Probably. But it would cut your commission substantially."

Anne shrugged. "No problem. I can handle it. I'll make up for it later on."

"Right on! I'll see to it that you do."

Thanks to Anne's willingness to sacrifice to help Alex Johns reach his goal, the sales quota was surpassed, and he got his bonus. What did Anne get in return? A great deal. In addition to her boss's appreciation and friendship, he knows that he owes her. Now, for example, when a particularly promising prospect calls to set up an appointment to test drive a new car, the manager is as likely as not to throw the business Anne's way. Or, as that old saying goes, "One hand washes the other." As another observer of the business scene once said, "Nothing is more profitable than a well-calculated sacrifice."

> "Nothing is more profitable than a well-calculated sacrifice."

ARE YOU IN A NO-WIN SITUATION?

Napoleon said, "Victory goes to the most persevering." And you've probably heard this before: "Hang tough. A winner never quits, a quitter never wins."

Don't believe them. When the time to quit is right, the quitter wins.

■ Alice In Blunderland

Florida *Sun-Sentinel* career columnist Lona O'Connor counsels: "If your work life is that bad, your ultimate goal should be to change it for the better. That may mean transferring or changing your job altogether."

Know Your Boss

How well do *you* know your boss? Do you understand his or her special problems and needs? Can you answer the following questions?

- How ambitious is your boss? What's his or her next step up the ladder?

- Can you help him in any way to achieve his career or departmental objectives?

- Can you pinpoint and help eliminate the operation's productivity roadblocks?

- Is there any constructive action you can take to boost your company's bottom line?

- Are there any personnel conflicts you can help alleviate?

- If your boss is overworked, as almost all bosses are, can you come up with any ideas to help reduce his or her workload?

- A major supervisory responsibility is to safeguard the safety and well-being of employees. Do you have any ideas that will make the workplace less hazardous?

- Are four of your favorite words, "How can I help?"

- Are two of your favorite words, "No problem!"?

How many questions can you add to this list?

Alice was as mixed up as a chocolate cake before it's poured into the pan. Little wonder. Anyone in that chaotic work environment would be tearing her hair out or worse. The problem was, well, impossible to define, and that's always a problem. Step one in solving any problem is to define it. Everything started to go sour six months ago when Alice's boss, the founder of the gourmet restaurant where she worked, died of a heart attack. The boss's son Maurice, who had been working as the overpaid maitre d', had taken over after his father's death. Unfortunately, he knew little about running a restaurant. Alice, who handled the books and served at the cash register, watched the business fall apart and found herself in a quandary that was turning into a nightmare.

Profits were declining precipitously. The bartender was skimming outrageously. First one chef quit, then another. Loyal customers were deserting. Maurice, who acted like he was the last word on restaurant management, accused everyone including Alice of "robbing him blind." As Alice tearfully complained to her husband, she was the only one who *wasn't* cheating him.

"So for Pete's sake," her husband barked, "who needs it!"

That's the point exactly. The restaurant was doomed. Chapter 11 was imminent. It was a just matter of time before the business folded. Alice was in a no-win situation. The only sensible decision she could make was to quit. The longer she took to act on that decision, the more aggravation she would get and the more she would hurt her career. Five months after Alice quit, so did the business. Today Maurice is a waiter, while Alice is happily employed by a catering business.

What About You?

Are you an unfortunate victim in a faltering enterprise—in a no-win predicament you are unable to remedy through no fault of your own? Should you hang in there like a hero or fly the coop like a smart bird? A good way to evaluate your situation is to borrow one of the oldest and most effective consultant's tools you could name. Take a blank sheet of paper and draw a line down the center. Label the left side of the sheet "pro" and the right side "con." On the "pro" side list all the benefits and common sense reasons you can think of to hang on to your job. On the "con" side enter all the reasons you should quit. Go over the two lists to make sure you included every pertinent consideration. Then, on a scale of 1 to 5, rank each item listed by its importance. The rest is a simple matter of arithmetic. If the "pro's" outscore the "con's," stick; if they don't, quit.

"YOU CANNOT SERVE TWO MASTERS." SEZ WHO?

It's bad enough to have one boss working against you. Get more than one on your enemies list and, from a career standpoint at least, you're not long for this world.

But as Carol Kleiman, Jobs columnist for the *Chicago Tribune*, points out, "Working for multiple bosses can mean multiple headaches or multiple praise. It depends on you."

■ Rose's Strategy

A year ago Rose M. was a member of her textile company's secretarial pool. A tiny pea in a crowded pod. Today she's Administrative Assistant to the Executive Vice President with a foot in middle management's door. Here's why.

Says Rose, "Let's assume, for example, that you report to two bosses. A common dilemma you face is to keep both of them happy when they both need your services at the same time. Whose request do you favor? That of Boss A or Boss B? The seemingly obvious answer is the one in the senior position. But it isn't that simple."

Rose explains why. Keeping Boss A happy at the expense of Boss B is anything but an ideal solution. The smart strategy is to take steps to keep all superiors off your list of enemies. Whether you have two, three, or more bosses, the trick is to make certain that no one feels slighted. "It's really not that difficult," Rose says. If her strategy had a name, she adds, it would be called "passing the buck." Instead of Rose making the whose-request-to-honor-first decision, she lets the brass make it for her.

> "Whether you have two, three, or more bosses, the trick is to make certain that no one feels slighted."

The trick in determining what projects get priority, she adds, is to first pinpoint the project's urgency then set priorities accordingly. She cites an example from her days in the secretarial pool. Boss number one (we'll call him Mr. Jones) came to her with a rush request to prepare a report right away. As she was about to get started, boss number two (Ms. Smith) approached her desk, urgency clouding her face. "Rose, I gotta have this spread sheet worked up yesterday." Rose wasn't flustered. She expressed personal concern about Ms. Smith's assignment, then informed her of Mr. Jones's rush order and asked if she would please check with Mr. Jones and let her know which job to do first.

"I couldn't refuse either assignment," Rose explains, "but I had to know which one was more important, and that wasn't my place to decide."

President Harry Truman was famous for having a plaque on his desk that read: THE BUCK STOPS HERE. Waiting until you're the boss before making the buck stop at your desk is good advice to keep in mind when you report to multiple bosses. If you have more than one boss, evaluate every decision you have to make with all of your bosses in mind.

ESCAPE STRATEGY:
HOW TO GET RID OF A TOXIC BOSS

You wouldn't eat a bun drenched in arsenic. So why swallow a despicable boss's toxic abuse? Yet thousands of victimized employees eat toxic crow on the job every day. Toxic bosses come in a variety of shapes, sizes, and forms. They make life miserable and the job unrewarding for a countless number of unhappy, held-back employees. In today's marketplace, with shortages of skilled workers creating countless job openings in so many industries, sitting still for abuse is dumber than crossing the street blindfolded. Are you being victimized by a toxic boss? Check to determine if any of the following abuses ring a bell with you in regard to your workplace:

- Sexual harassment. Repeated propositions in the face of rejection. Butt patting, unwanted hugging, sexually offensive language.
- Unreasonable work pressures, unfair work overload.
- Unfairly being bypassed for deserved merit increases.
- Underpaid because you are female—or in rare cases, male.
- The boss playing favorites, leaving you with the short end of the stick.
- Evidence of religious, racial, age, gender, or other bias.
- The boss seeks to involve you in unethical or illegal practices.
- Exposure to hazardous physical or mental health conditions.
- The boss fails to give you fair credit for your profit-boosting ideas.

If You Are Victimized, What Can You Do About It?

Plenty, depending on the severity of the abuse. First discuss the situation with your boss. *Perhaps* he or she doesn't even realize the behavior is unacceptable. If the situation doesn't improve, follow the next three steps.

1. Take your case to a higher level executive.
2. Try getting a transfer to another department or division.
3. As a last measure, inform your boss that unless he ceases it, you will bring his unacceptable behavior to public attention. Remember, this is an extreme step, and before you take it you should get evidence (if possible) and do research. Do things such as get legal advice, talk to your union representative, or find out if this has ever happened to anyone else in the company. When you are prepared to do battle, the boss may just turn and run.

But, what if your boss is *the* top executive or owner and all appeals for fair treatment fail? In that case, your best course of action may be to seek greener and more honorable pastures for your own peace of mind and self respect—not to mention your income and outcome.

CHAPTER LESSONS

✓ No one is more important to your income and career advancement than your direct supervisor.

✓ Assess the situation. Are you responsible for your boss's negative feelings because you aren't putting your all into the work? Remember, doing your job well and thoroughly benefits you.

✓ Once your attitude pits you against your boss, your career is doomed.

✓ Improving a bad attitude will improve your status in the workplace.

✓ Listen to your inner "get-ahead responses" to stagnant situations and act on them.

✓ If you hate your boss, identify why and find a way to deal with the problem. Otherwise, it may be time to move on.

✓ To get along with your boss, you need to understand his needs and goals and help him meet them. In short, **Know Thy Boss.**

✓ Learn to recognize—and exit—a no-win situation when you see it.

✓ Learn to recognize a toxic business atmosphere and/or boss—and get out quickly.

CHAPTER 8:
THE WRONG JOB

PROBLEM: You Picked the Wrong Employer
Rx: Make a Quick and Smart Switch

"No man, properly occupied, was ever miserable."
—L. E. Landon, Author

■ Darcy Doesn't Work Here Anymore

Darcy receives all kinds of recognition and appreciation for her job as an executive assistant to the company's president. All kinds but one—money! Her husband, Chet, keeps bugging her. "Honey, the paycheck you get is a crime."

Tightlipped, Darcy replies, "There's nothing I can do about it. The company can't afford to give me an increase."

"Bull!" Chet scoffs.

"It's not bull," she insists.

"Okay, then do me a favor. Talk to your father."

Darcy's dad is a well paid executive. Darcy reluctantly seeks his advice. "Chet says my boss could give me a raise if he wanted to."

"Okay, let's find out," her father replies, and checks out her employer.

"Chet's wrong," Dad informs her the next day. "Your company is on a very tight budget. But Chet's absolutely right that you are outrageously underpaid for the job you do. Your company ranks low in its field and is going downhill. If I were you, I'd get out while the getting is good."

The advice Darcy's dad offers makes sense. People pick the wrong employer for any number of reasons. Why? A sudden turn in the economy that causes the company's failure in the marketplace is just one of them. There are scores of other reasons, but they are not always so clear.

As in Darcy's case, quitting a job at a company going downhill may seem like the obvious solution: You picked the wrong employer. So you quit and get out. But it may not be as easy as it sounds. Untold thousands of workers, concluding that they made a bad choice, jump ship too hastily and wind up worse off than before. However green other pastures may seem, you should never make a job-switching decision without considered forethought and careful analysis.

The smart strategy when wanderlust strikes is to ask yourself the following questions:

◆　What bugs me so much about my employer that I'm ready to sacrifice whatever seniority credits I've accumulated?

◆　Is there anything I can do to improve my situation that might make more sense than jumping ship?

THINK TWICE, THEN ONCE AGAIN

Before chancing a leap into the unknown, take the following short quiz. The more objective your answers, the more reasoned and helpful your conclusions will be.

(Note: If you do not own this copy of Job Smarts, *then be sure to make a photocopy of this quiz before you mark your answers.)*

	YES	NO

1. Are you angry and frustrated because you feel you're underpaid? Does your research lead you to believe you can earn more money elsewhere?   —— ——

2. Are you for one reason or another a victim of unequal treatment? Has anything convinced you another employer will treat you more fairly?   —— ——

3. Are you not being used to the best of your ability? Is there any action you can take to remedy this situation?   —— ——

4. Are you a victim of broken promises? Is there a higher level manager you can appeal to for justice?   —— ——

5. Are you being denied the training that could help you advance? Are you reasonably sure you will get the training you need elsewhere?   —— ——

6. Do you find it hard to get along with your coworkers? Could the problem possibly be your personality or temperament and not theirs?   —— ——

7. Are you outside the inner circle or "old boy" network? Is there an influential key person or two who could get you included?   —— ——

8. Do you hate the work you are doing? What assurances do you have that you would like some other work better?   —— ——

9. Do you feel a supervisor or coworker is taking unfair advantage of you? If so, are you in a position to do anything about it?   —— ——

10. Do you feel something shady or dishonest is going on?   —— ——

Total Number of YES Answers   ———

Enter the number of "yes" answers on the preceding page. If the total is two or less, think twice before doing anything drastic. Obviously, the more "yes" answers you record—and the less action you can take to reverse the situation—the more likely it appears that your best bet is to bid your present employer a not-so-fond adieu.

WHAT DO YOU DO FOR A LIVING?

The good news is that in today's job market the personnel scavengers will come to you on bended knee *if* you have needed skills and experience to offer. As a viable job candidate, you may be able to put yourself in the driver's seat if you play your cards right. To get into the driver's seat you'll need education, skills, real-life experience, and *a clear understanding of what type of job you want.* The U.S. economy grew at historically high rates in the last decade, particularly in the years 1998-2000. Although this growth is likely to slow at some point, your employment outlook can still be positive. According to the *Employment Outlook Survey* for the first quarter of 2001 conducted by Manpower Corporation, a leading employment services specialist, the hiring frenzy of the past few years may be slowing. However, what "slowing" means is that only 28 percent of the companies surveyed expected to do additional hiring. *Only 28 percent!* This is quite a large figure, and, as Manpower concludes, "substantial staffing remains to be done."

It's no secret, of course, that college grads have the edge in the job market. But unprecedented opportunities exist for high school grads as well, and especially for high school grads who earn college or vocational school credits part time. Prospective employers admire the initiative this effort shows.

Companies, profit and nonprofit, are on the offensive as never before for skilled and productive workers. What it boils down to is that these days there is a fairly large onus on employers to find ways to keep workers happy on the job with their proverbial noses fixed to the grindstone—or else. Are you happy at *your* job? If not, it may interest you to know that the "or else" alternative is being increasingly exercised by millions of talented and well-trained young people who are either dissatisfied at work and/or convinced they can do better.

If you zero in on the market's demand, make sure you know your stuff, and show up at the right place at the right time, then landing a good job was never easier. The outlook is especially bright for grads looking to launch their career, for ambitious climbers seeking to change their employers, for young people with enough evidence and self-confidence to convince prospective employers they are worth more than they are presently getting, and for working mothers who require not only respectable incomes but enough flexibility to fulfill their family responsibilities. Let's look at the story of Anna Mae Linden for an example.

■ Don't Take No For an Answer

Anna Mae is a young mother of 24, with computer science skills that she developed at a part-time job while in college, on her own computer at home, and in two years on the job after earning her BS degree. She didn't work at a high tech company, but Anna Mae had a key job in the data processing department. If a machine caught a bug, got hung up for one reason or another, or a new procedure had to be devised, Anna Mae was the one the department invariably called upon. That was fine. The complexities of technology intrigued her. She met challenges with enthusiasm. She liked her job, her boss liked her, and she won the respect of everyone in the company.

There was only one thing she didn't like. Because her husband Ted was working long hours to launch his law career, and her work schedule was rigid, it was becoming increasingly difficult for Anna Mae to handle both her job and her responsibilities for her two-year-old daughter. Pondering the situation, Anna Mae was convinced her problem could be solved without too much difficulty. Her situation wasn't unique. She approached Mr. Durkin, her boss, with this thought in mind.

"Most of my work," she pointed out, "can be done as easily at home as in the office. I have a computer and the necessary software, and with email at my fingertips, it would be no problem at all to adjust my hours to both the company's and my family's needs. It would be no loss to the company, and beneficial to me."

Her behind-the-times boss's response was a frown. "I don't know," he replied, "I don't think flextime would work in this company."

"I don't see why it wouldn't in my case," Anna Mae persisted. "Will you please give it some thought?"

Mr. Durkin promised to do so. A week later she approached him again. "Have you given—?"

"Yes, I have," her boss interrupted. "I don't think it would work. Also, I wouldn't want to set a precedent."

Anna Mae didn't push it. "Thank you for your consideration," she replied curtly.

Three weeks after that, following the two weeks notice that she had given, she was gone.

One evening five weeks later she received a call at home from Mr. Durkin.

"I have good news, Anna Mae. I've been able to work out a flex-time arrangement for you that I think will be very much to your liking."

"Thanks for your trouble," she replied politely, "but I'm well established in a new job that I think will be *more* to my liking."

As a wise person once said: "When you gotta go, you gotta go."

Turtle Soup

Fact I—For years now we have been living through a hiring bonanza that has changed the way people work.

Fact II—As former Labor Secretary Robert Reich concedes, "Loyalty is dead." Well, if not dead, slowly strangling.

Fact III—On top of the hiring bonanza, we are living through a firing bonanza as well. Downsizing, firing, restructuring pick your own descriptive term. According to outplacement specialists Challenger, Gray & Christmas, a record number of employees are receiving pink slips.

What it adds up to is *un*certain times with a capital *UN*. What uncertain times add up to is worry, spelled F-E-A-R.

For a good way to confront fear head-on, review Fact I above. In recent years work methods have been transformed as never before. One of the major effects of the transformation, thanks in large measure to the computer, is the flextime phenomenon taking hold in many companies. Another widespread development is the growing number of freelancers or independent contractors. As *Newsweek* writer Richard Turner states, "many companies are increasingly eager to give people work *without giving them jobs.*"

A Cleveland employment manager puts it this way: "Many personnel people still haven't responded to the reality that in some situations work can be done as effectively, and often more economically, at home than in the office or plant. It's simply a matter of efficient work measurement, then deciding what is best for all parties concerned."

As a result many gutsy employees, either fearful of being bounced or disenchanted with their jobs, are setting themselves up as contractual workers at home and offering their services to the highest bidder. A computer programmer we know doubled his income this way, and says, "For the first time in years I feel really secure."

Admittedly, there is risk involved in such a move. But for those with marketable skills, the risk is far less than you might imagine. In the hot fields in particular (as we shall see) there are bosses clamoring to fill job openings. So as a wise observer once stated the case:

> "Behold the turtle. He makes
> progress only when he sticks his neck out."
> —James Conant, Educator

CAN YOU AFFORD TO
DO WHAT YOU WANT TO DO?

You may be able to learn something from one of my own work experiences. More years ago than I like to remember, I had a good job doing systems work for Faberge Perfumes Inc. in Ridgefield, New Jersey. I had about 20 people working for me. But even though my income was respectable, my career growth potential was good, and I was fortunate enough to report to a great boss, I was dissatisfied. The reason was simple. For one thing, I didn't particularly enjoy systems work. For another, I didn't like supervising a lot of people, most of whom were less conscientious than I was. Most important of all, what I *really* wanted to do was write.

I had written a few articles and stories that were well received. But at the time I had two small children to support and a home to maintain. Even though I had proven I could write for commercial publications, I couldn't afford to give up a steady income for the uncertain existence of a freelance writer.

What to do? I spell out the story in detail in a recently published book of mine called *Achieving Financial Independence As a Freelance Writer* (Blue Heron Publishing Company, Portland, OR). But I'll summarize one of the main highlights here. I continued writing, mostly evenings and weekends, and expanded my markets, until my income from writing amounted to about a third of what I earned at Faberge. (Needless to say, I worked my butt off in the process, but I have always maintained that anything in life that's worth getting is worth working hard for.)

My next step was to find myself a part-time writing job working two days a week for a small public relations agency. At this point my combined income from freelance work and the part time job amounted to about 75 percent of my Faberge' income. When I announced to my boss that I was resigning, his initial response was to call me crazy. "In time," he told me, "you could become financial vice president of this company." I never confided to him that should I attain this noble distinction, the job would create a a nightmare existence for me. I wasn't cut out for that kind of work.

Within a year or so I was able to quit the part-time job, and the P.R. agency became one of my best clients. I never became rich as a freelance writer. Maybe some day I will, but that's not what really matters. Still, I did become financially independent, a shade more than comfortable, and—most importantly—*I was doing what I wanted to do!* As as old Blue Eyes might have put it, "I did it my way!"

It is impossible to determine how many people—right now, at this very minute—are afraid to quit jobs they don't like to take a shot at what they would much rather do because they can't afford to give up a reliable income. But if by some chance you can relate to the situation, work up your courage, find creative ways to meet your financial requirements and, when you feel you're ready, make a part-time transition. To kill an alligator, you don't go for its jaw at the outset. You grab it by the tail and gradually work your way to its head. Gradually changing jobs worked for me; it can work for you.

What If the Problem Is Your Boss?

Unlike my situation at Faberge where, I had a great boss, but didn't care for my work, a young high school grad I know enjoyed his work immensely. We'll call this young man "George." Now, George was a computer maven and gaining more skills every day. The owner of the company where George worked billed himself as a Computer Consultant, and he had three computer gurus (including George) working for him. George doesn't like to use profanity, but if he did, his boss would surely qualify. To put it in printable language, his boss was a cheap, cheating, chiseling, penny pincher. Maybe that's why his firm's turnover was so great.

George, however, was in no position to quit in a huff. He had a pregnant wife and a year-old daughter to support, as well as a bankbook with less than four figures. On top of that, he was taking advanced computer science courses at a nearby tech school. He struggled just to keep his head above water.

As the saying goes, "desperate times call for desperate measures." To make ends meet, George began taking on freelance work. He didn't steal any of his boss's clients, but he did manage to find a few of his own on the side. In time, and as George's knowledge and experience grew, so did his customer roster and income. It finally reached the point where he was able to confront his boss with a deal: "Two days a week at the same rate of pay."

His boss hemmed and hawed; however, he had no choice but to accept. George was too valuable to him. Just like my own experience, before long he was in a position to tell his boss, "Don't call me, I'll call you," and he opened shop of his own. At last word, George's income exceeded $200,000 a year and there are four people on *his* payroll.

THE MORALITY FACTOR

A production manager employed by a major auto manufacturer approached a top-level marketing vice president one day. The manager had an anxious frown on his face. "What's the problem?" the VP asked. The manager called his attention to an engine defect and explained a correction would delay production and cost several thousand dollars to complete. He pointed out that a serious safety hazard was involved.

The vice president brushed him off. "Don't worry about it; I'll take care of it."

His reply didn't satisfy the production manager. "Sir, if the engine overheats—"

The marketing executive, whose major concern was keeping to the schedule, cut him short. "Let me worry about quality. You keep pushing those vehicles out."

The production manager resigned the next day. What would you have done in his shoes? Blow the whistle? Go over the VP's head? Or, as this manager did, simply quit?

When we are faced with situations that go against our morals and ethics, we must make highly personal decisions.

Your personal code of behavior is between you and your conscience. So it's up to you to decide: Would you work for a company that is guilty of dishonest or unethical conduct? Or for a boss who engages in shady shenanigans? Apart from the stirrings of conscience, you need to keep the legal factor in mind. Suppose that, in addition to his own dishonest behavior, your boss seeks to get you involved? Or has already done so? If so, keep in mind that just because your boss is the major perpetrator in a dishonest enterprise it doesn't mean you get off the hook. You could wind up being his cell mate. So does it make sense to stick around? Innumerable cases can be cited in which employers, not only swindled customers, consumers, or stockholders, but they also fixed the evidence so that a subordinate wound up being the patsy.

What follows is a rundown of cases derived from a consultant's files in which a subordinate's "reason for leaving," most commonly unpublicized, was related to a company's or executive's dishonest or improper behavior of one kind or another. Scroll down the list on the next page and note the items that remind you of your own organization and should ring alarm bells.

◆ Customers who are cheated—short-changed, over-charged, given the wrong product, and so forth

◆ The cover-up of defective products or approval of such products.

◆ Greedy doctors who perform useless or questionable procedures on patients for the profit they can make out of it.

◆ Insurance companies or HMOs that deny customers procedures that they are entitled to rightfully.

◆ Executives who secretly handle their own personal business on company time.

◆ Stock brokers who give clients worthless tips in an effort to increase business and commissions.

◆ Builders who produce shoddy homes or fail to perform promised construction or repair work.

◆ Insurers who misrepresent coverage to gullible customers.

◆ Companies that pollute the environment.

◆ Companies that refuse to eliminate hazardous conditions because of the cost involved.

The list could go on. Hapless folks are swindled a hundred ways from Sunday every day of the week. Victims may range from single parents in tight financial straits to people with disabilities to the trusting elderly to you and me. Some people can justify working for employers who are guilty of dishonest or antisocial behavior. Others cannot or, if already employed, feel uncomfortable with or ashamed by their association.

But keep in mind that actions or omissions don't necessarily have to be illegal to turn off many people. A friend of the family confided to me not long ago, "I can't take it any more." She referred to her job with a pharmaceutical company where products were priced outrageously high to improve the company's bottom line, while those whose lives depended on the medication were forced to spend $120 per month to get it. Some could not afford such an expense and were forced to chose between putting food on the table or drugs in their mouth. The woman ended up resigning.

Two more examples: My daughter quit a high-paying job with a major tobacco company some time ago because she could no longer stand being part of an enterprise that made a product that caused heart trouble, cancer, and emphysema. A young man fresh out of college, the son of a friend, left a promising trainee's job because, in his own words, "I was embarrassed by the company's poor reputation and low level of customer service. I was ashamed to tell people I worked there."

Experience shows that in companies most sensitive to the importance of outstanding customer service, not only are customers happier and more loyal, but employees are as well.

"It's extremely important," says Edith Morgan, a New York-based job counselor, "for workers to feel pride in the work they do, the department they're in, the organization that employs them. Failing such pride, or worse, feeling ashamed of one's job, I can think of no better impetus to start shopping the market."

The "Feel Good" Factor

Job satisfaction is a two-way street. As an employee, half the responsibility for job satisfaction is yours. Your obligation is to be honest, ethical, and conscientious and to give your boss a fair day's work for a fair day's pay. Your employer is, or should be, equally responsible for generating a "feel good" state of mind among workers. How conscientious is your employer in fulfilling this part of the bargain? Take the following short quiz to find out.

	YES	NO
1. Is your boss receptive to your special need to deviate from rigid "9 to 5" hours?	___	___
2. Does your employer give fair and equal treatment to all employees regardless of race, religion, gender, age, etc.?	___	___
3. Does your boss compliment you when you do a good job?	___	___
4. Does your boss display an interest in your personal and family problems and needs?	___	___
5. Does your employer provide adequate opportunities and training to ensure your personal development and growth?	___	___
6. Does your boss take time occasionally to chat with you on subjects that are not business related?	___	___
7. Does your boss seek your advice and opinion from time to time?	___	___
8. Are your boss's job instructions clear and detailed enough?	___	___
9. Does your boss periodically let you know how you are doing with improvement and not just criticism in mind?	___	___
10. Does your boss sound you out from time to time about any complaints, problems, or unfulfilled needs you might have?	___	___

Total Number of YES Answers _____

How Does Your Employer Rate? Enter the total number of "yes" answers in the space provided above. In determining whether or not your employer helps you to feel good on the job, apply the following general guidelines: 8 or more "yes's"— Excellent, 7—Good, 6—Above average, 5—Average. Any score below 5—Draw your own conclusion.

SHOULD YOU PUT IN YOUR TWO CENTS?

Sometimes there are things you like about your job: the money, your boss, the people you work with, along with things you don't like: a product, the training program, compensation you feel is not fair and equal. You hate the thought of giving up the good things, but you feel your career's future will be stunted if you can't do something about the bad things. Where do you go from here?

Remember the turtle? Depending on how much the negative aspects of your job bother you, the time could be right for sticking your neck out.

At least that's the way Susie S. looked at it. Reasoning, "I have nothing to lose," she decided to stick out her neck. Susie enjoyed her job as an associate financial planner. She found the work exciting and challenging. But she was aggravated by the way the department was run. Mr. Morse seemed to operate on the principle that if he didn't personally direct and administer every last detail of a project the job wouldn't be done right. He peered over the shoulders of everyone he supervised like a nervous owl. Only last week Susie had cut into one of his long, drawn-out instructions. "Mr. Morse, I *know* how it works. I've done it before. Several times." His close scrutiny of every detail was driving her crazy, and this morning he had done it again.

Sticking her neck out might cost her her job, Susie realized. But she decided it was worth the risk. Approaching her boss's desk, she said, "Mr. Morse, can I speak with you in private?"

He frowned. "Why, uh, yes, of course."

They went to the small conference room where Susie spelled out her feelings. "You don't give me a chance to think for myself," she complained, "and I'm not the only one who feels this way. I like working here, but sometimes you make me feel like a third-grade kid. I'm about ready to quit."

"Oh, please don't do that, Susie. I had no idea you felt this way." Mr. Morse nodded thoughtfully. "Thank you for confiding in me."

Instead of firing her, Susie's boss developed a sensitivity to her feelings. Sometimes brashness pays off. Her job was never more enjoyable.

Putting in your two cents—saying what you think and risking your job—doesn't always work. But when used as a last resort when you feel you have nothing to lose, expressing your frustrations could make sense and lead to positive change. Here are a few other examples of workers who stuck their necks out and prospered.

■ Bob

Bob, a utility worker in a manufacturing plant, was told as part of a job to climb a high scaffolding that he thought was a safety hazard. His boss, a maintenance department group leader, declared the structure was safe and refused to have it repaired or inspected. Although Bob needed the job, he would rather quit than take a chance with his health. Quitting, however, was a last resort option. Instead, he went over his boss's head to talk to the maintenance foreman. When the supervisor checked the condition of the scaffolding, he not only decided it should be repaired, but he also fired the group leader for negligence.

■ Eleanor

Eleanor's boss, the controller, was running an illicit gambling business on company time. Part of her job included keeping records and conducting transactions for the gambling business. Eleanor became increasingly uneasy about her role in the enterprise and told her boss she could no longer do it. "Then I take it you're giving notice," he replied coldly. That's not what Eleanor had in mind. She blew the whistle instead, and now her boss is giving notice.

■ Charley

Charley's employer, a textile importer, consistently over-billed customers or short-shipped merchandise. Since Charley was in the billing department, the dishonesty nagged at his conscience even though it wasn't his idea. When he complained about the practice he was fired. "No great loss," he wife said. "With your experience you'll have no problem getting a job in an honest enterprise."

The point of these stories is clear. When you feel you have a moral or ethical dilemma and you can't work under these conditions, speak your mind.

FOLLOW THE MONEY

How important is money to you? English author Henry Fielding wrote, "Make money your god, and it will plague you like the devil." True, but there is a difference between making money your god and earning the maximum income you are capable of and entitled to.

Sometimes the "wrong employer" can be a *good* employer but not be able to meet your financial needs.

Sometimes, even though you get fulfillment and satisfaction from a job, an opportunity arises with another employer willing to pay you more. When that happens, whether or not to take advantage of it can be a tough decision to make.

Do any of these situations sound familiar to you? Would you like to know how your salary stacks up against competitive enterprises in your industry and location? Do some research. Ask around. Or check with Salary.com (http://www.salary.com) on the Internet. It may provide some enlightenment. (See the box below for a comprehensive list of salary related Web sites.)

SALARY SITES ON THE WORLD WIDE WEB

■ America's Career InfoNet (http://www.acinet.org)

■ Economic Research Institute (http://www.erieri.com/doltrends)

■ Realrates.com (http://www.realrates.com/)

■ U.S. Bureau of Labor Statistics/Occupational Employment Statistics (http://stats.bls.gov/oesnl/oes_alph.htm)

■ U.S. Department of Labor/*Occupational Outlook Handbook* (http://www.bls.gov/ocohome.htm)

■ Wageweb (http://www.wageweb.com/)

■ Bernie's Decision

Four years after earning his business administration degree, Marketing Associate Bernie Rollins, age 26, had a secure, well-paying job with a medium-size toy company. But "well paying" is a matter of judgment. Bernie had started harboring doubts. Earning $48,000 a year wasn't bad for someone his age; but, with a family to support, it wasn't great either. So Bernie wisely decided to have a closer look at the pros and cons of staying in his job.

The pros were impressive. Bernie's boss, a senior vice president, was a great guy to work for. Bernie got along well with his coworkers. He had made some good friends in the department. The plant was located within half an hour of his home. And, most importantly, Bernie enjoyed what he did and looked forward to coming to work in the morning. Those were the plusses, at least the most important ones.

As for the cons, the main problem was money. For a college grad with four years of work experience $48,000 a year was a respectable salary, Bernie reasoned. But for a top-performing professional, it wasn't spectacular. With a two-year-old in the crib and another baby on the way, Bernie felt his bank balance was growing slower than hair on a bowling ball. What bothered Bernie even more, though, was that his boss was only 38, with no sign of retirement in sight. On top of that, two other people in Marketing were higher on the career ladder than he was. He would get small raises from year to year, but it was a matter of simple arithmetic to determine that he'd be a long time in line for promotion to project manager or vice president. There was a lot of wheel spinning in store for him. So when Bernie ran into a college classmate who had a similar job, he asked about salary ranges. The friend informed him he was knocking down $66,000 a year at his large company and had the chance of becoming a VP. Naturally, Bernie's ears perked up.

His wife Martha's ears perked up as well. "You'd be giving up a lot," she agreed, "but look how much you can gain."

Bernie nodded thoughtfully. "Okay, honey, I'm outta there."

What Do You Value Most?

In making a career decision, what do you value most? Over 2,000 students across the United States responded to this question in a Jobtrak.com survey. Here are their responses:

Balancing Work & Life   42 percent
Money   26 percent
Advancement Potential   23 percent
Location   9 percent

What do *you* value most? If you are presently employed, does your job satisfy what is most important to you? It is interesting, and perhaps significant, that "Job Security" does not appear on the above list. This is not surprising in today's job market. **When you consider a possible change, don't overlook smaller companies.**

"Many young job seekers," says Connecticut career counselor Lester Lewis, "target their sights on giant corporations where downsizing is unpredictable, ignoring small manufacturers and commercial firms that are crying out for skilled people and don't know where to find them."

Lester Lewis points out that while the small companies may be less glamorous than the giants and often offer lower starting salaries, from the standpoint of work/life balance, advancement potential, and location, the smaller companies often have the larger ones beat. In job hunting he recommends running the gamut—check out small, medium, and large companies.

What you value most may not appear on the list above at all. Dan G. is an ambitious young engineering graduate with an active imagination that brims over with ideas. "When I was job hunting six months ago," he says, "a value as important to me as money was my prospective employer's innovational or entrepreneurial climate. It would devastate me to work for an organization that brushed me off when I had an idea to suggest or a boss who kept saying, 'We can't try it because the budget's too tight.'"

Dan found employment with an aggressive, small firm manned by staffers who are all under 30. A project that was the result of a brainstorm of Dan's is now on the front burner and appears to have good money-making potential. If the project works out as he hopes, his income will skyrocket.

Conclusion: Job hunting is a highly individualized proposition.

FISH WHERE THE BIG ONES ARE BITING

There's no point in fishing for fresh water salmon in a salty pool. Thousands (millions?) of people are underpaid, not because their employers are uncaring and cheap, but because either: A—They are stuck in jobs with little or no growth potential, or B—The company's fortunes are fading and what they're paid is all management can afford. So, especially if your talent and inclination lean toward technology, it makes sense to train up to the hilt and set your sights on the big money offers.

It's no surprise to anyone that the best opportunities in the new millennium are computer-related where the talent shortfall is most sharply felt. Today corporations are playing tug of war in the fight to get highly trained workers. With global markets and increasing dependence on technology, it is no wonder that companies pay well for computer engineers, software specialists, systems analysts, database scientists, desktop publishing mavens, Web site designers, and the like. These workers are building the kind of bankrolls in a year or two that took Dad a decade or more to accumulate.

According to a recent Information Technology Association of America survey, about 1.6 million high-tech personnel will be needed over the next year in addition to the 10 million already employed.

Apart from information technology, hot occupations—where entry-level salaries often run upwards of $40,000—include: mechanical engineer, physician assistant, financial services broker, and marketing specialist. This is just a sampling of hot jobs to whet your appetite. See the sidebar below for more information. Or check the dozens of job-related sites on the Web for a more detailed analysis.

OCCUPATIONS WITH FAST GROWTH AND HIGH STARTING SALARIES

Occupation	Employment Growth	Starting Salary
Civil Engineers	21 percent	$39,852
Computer Engineers	99 percent	$53,443
Computer Programmers	30 percent	$51,581
Computer Systems Analysts	99 percent	$51,581
Economics and Finance Workers	41 percent	$40,297
Electrical and Electronics Engineers	26 percent	$50,850
Mechanical Engineers	16 percent	$48,340
Occupational Therapists	34 percent	$30,850*
Physician Assistants	48 percent	$57,648**
Registered Nurses	22 percent	$33,452

Sources: U.S. Department of Labor, National Association of Colleges and Employers, Winter 2001 Salary Survey, except:

*Occupational Outlook Handbook

**American Academy of Physician Assistants 1999 Census Survey

The good news is that, according to latest reports, recent college grads who display the kind of talent companies want, don't seem to be held back by their lack of experience. The *hard* news is that if your hopes are set on landing an entry-level job paying $40,000 and you expect to earn even more over time, don't consider yourself "educated" if you've gone no further than high school. In the new millennium, when you stop learning, you move backwards.

CHAPTER LESSONS

✓ If you want to make big bucks, enter a field such as engineering, technology, or health care.

✓ Look before you leap. Think and plan before you jump from a poor work environment to an unknown environment.

✓ We are in the midst of a hiring and firing bonanza. In short, the job market is volatile and highly skilled, highly educated workers will have the best job security.

✓ Speak your mind if you feel your job places you in an ethical bind and you can't work under these conditions.

✓ Learn what you value the most: money or other life factors, such as advancement opportunities, the ability to learn new skills and grow, location, work environment, family considerations. Then shape your career plan to match these values.

✓ Many people are underpaid simply because they are stuck in jobs with little or no growth potential or at companies that have seen their better days.

CHAPTER 9:
LEARN TO APPRECIATE
THE BOTTOM LINE

PROBLEM: You Are Not Bottom-Line Oriented
Rx: Become an Ace Problem Solver

Profit is the main and ultimate goal of business. If your goal is to
climb the corporate ladder, see to it that every action you take, every
decision you make, enhances the bottom line of the enterprise. If you do this
and fail to advance, you are either in the wrong job or the wrong organization.
—Philip Brass, Executive Vice President (Ret.), Faberge Cosmetics

"All griping does is turn you grumpy," Al's boss told him with annoyance. Al, a billing machine operator, was bright, well educated, and hardworking. He had just complained about the lousy break he felt he was getting—no promotion in three years, and no prospect of advancement.

His boss snorted, "Opportunities grow like crabgrass around here. All you have to do is keep your eyes open."

"Like where?" Al replied.

"Here, I'll show you." His boss pulled out a newsletter announcing a Company-Wide Suggestion Program. "Do you want the lowdown about winning cash prizes and getting promoted? I can think of no better example than my own. I made department head two years ago because of an idea that I had submitted for improving the billing system. Profit-based ideas are career builders. That goes for all employees from entry level right up to the top. No opportunity? Don't believe it. All you have to do is use your eyes—and your head."

Labor leader Samuel Gompers said, "The worst roadblock for working people is the company that fails to make a profit."

> "In the workplace *problem* is a synonym for *opportunity.*"

The biggest favor working people can do for themselves is to contribute to profit performance. Opportunities abound if you look for them. Anything at all that hinders or blocks the making of profit provides you with a career building opportunity: Problems, bottlenecks, customer complaints, conditions that create machine trouble or tool malfunction, personnel conflicts—all erode profit and offer you the chance to come up with a good idea for stopping the erosion. Every one of these is an opportunity waiting for an ambitious employee to take advantage of it. In the workplace *problem* is a synonym for *opportunity.*

■ Anita and Myrna

Too bad Anita Phillips, a computer programmer, didn't understand that about problems. One day Brad Ravich, an accounts receivable department supervisor, approached Anita with a frown on his face.

"What's the problem?" she asked. "You look like your best friend just moved to Honolulu."

"That's how I feel," Brad replied. He held a report in his hand. "I can't get these darned columns to line up right when Special Deals are involved. If you could alter or rearrange the programming to accommodate them, it would make my life easier."

Anita glanced at the report. "I wish I could help you, Brad, but I'm tied up at the moment. I'll try to get to it this afternoon if I can."

She could have too, if she hadn't forgotten about it. In the meantime the supervisor, pressed to complete the report, asked another programmer, Myrna Davis, for help. Myrna was no less busy than Anita, but she took the time to oblige.

When Brad submitted the report to Milton Rubin, a Vice President, the executive said, "I see you managed to overcome that bugaboo with the Special Deals. What happened?"

"Myrna Davis helped me out. She revised the software to accommodate the Special Deals." When Brad left the office, Mr. Rubin picked up the phone and called Myrna. "That was a great job you did on that report. Thanks."

Myrna's problem-solving assistance and the executive's acknowledgement of it isn't going to make her a VP overnight. But it is a notch in her career belt, a notch Anita might have earned had she understood the value of pitching in to help solve problems. Actually, when you think about it, all job advancement comes from is the accumulation of enough notches on your career belt over a period of time.

WHERE DO YOU STAND?

How does *your* contribution to company profits affect your personal development and financial growth on the job? Employees at all levels fall into one of the three following categories of job performance: *Simple Negative, Simple Positive,* or *Special Elite.*

Simple Negative

These are the workers who just barely get by or whose performance is substandard. They do the minimum amount of work they can get by with and consider "goofing-off" to be outsmarting the boss and a personal accomplishment. They have poor attendance, take prolonged work breaks, and have attitudes that leave something to be desired. They must be monitored constantly, and their work double checked.

Their Prospects: They are bypassed for promotions and raises at wage review time. Liabilities to the organization, they are either not long for their employer or hang on by their teeth. People in this category wouldn't be reading this book.

Simple Positive

These men and women excel at their jobs and are essential contributors to corporate bottom-line growth. They are conscientious on a day-to-day basis, hardworking and dependable, and appreciated by their supervisors and coworkers. But they are not natural innovators or volunteers. They don't stand out from the crowd.

Their Prospects: These workers receive regular wage increases. They make slow and steady progress over weeks, months, or years, but they do not rocket to the top of the corporate ladder.

The Special Elite

These men and women stand out from the crowd. As innovators, volunteers, idea generators. They *aggressively* seek ways to solve problems, remove bottlenecks, and modify products and procedures to improve efficiency and generate increased company revenues.

Their Prospects: America's future executives and big money makers are found within this group. Smart management hungrily searches the marketplace and its own manpower pool for Special Elite performers, the men and women who grease corporate profit wheels and keep them turning.

Profits with People, Inc., a human resources consulting firm, reports that turnover rates at American corporations have reached a historic high. In the tech sector, more than 35 percent turn over 35 percent of their workforce each year. In other industries turnover is in the 15 percent to 20 percent range. On its Web site, the firm suggests that brain power is more important than "plant and raw materials" in our new economy. In a nutshell, it is what's between your ears and how you use that knowledge that will determine the direction and shape of your career.

Where do *you* stand? Search your heart and mind. In which of the aforementioned categories do you rightly belong? Let's find out. Take the following quiz. Then score yourself at the end.

(Note: If you do not own this copy of Job Smarts, *then be sure to make a photocopy of this quiz before you mark your answers.)*

	YES	NO
1. Are you rarely late to or absent from work?	—	—
2. Do you have a good imagination?	—	—
3. Are you constructively dissatisfied with the progress you've been making?	—	—
4. When you observe a problem or bottleneck in your department do you make an effort to solve it?	—	—
5. Do you think ahead to where you will be five years from now?	—	—
6. Do you ever bad-mouth your organization or its executives?	—	—
7. Do you have a positive attitude?	—	—
8. Do you get along well with your coworkers?	—	—
9. Do you consider yourself to be a good team player?	—	—
10. Do you ever hog credit for coworkers' good ideas?	—	—
11. Do you ever make sacrifices to help out your boss in a spot?	—	—
12. Do you complain a lot?	—	—

	YES	NO
13. Are you a take charge person?	___	___
14. Do you consider yourself to be quick on the pickup?	___	___
15. Do you take advantage of every training opportunity you can?	___	___
16. Do you always look for the next assignment after completing a job?	___	___
17. Do you too often stretch work breaks beyond prescribed limits?	___	___
18. Do you respond well to positive criticism?	___	___
19. Do you feel you are doing the kind of work for which you are best suited?	___	___
20. Do you understand the role that your customers play in your company's profit performance?	___	___
Your Profit IQ	___	___

Figure Out Your Advancement Potential

Kidding yourself never pays off. The more honest and objective you can be in checking the above "yes" or "no" blanks, the more value you will get from this exercise.

Calculate your score as follows: Give yourself 5 points for each "no" answer checked for Questions 6, 10, 12, and 17. Score 5 points for each "yes" answer checked for all the remaining questions. Then total and insert your score in the "Your Profit IQ" blank above.

Now rate your advancement potential as a contributor to your company's bottom-line performance: Excellent, if your score is 80 or higher; Good if it's 75 or 70; Fair if it's 65; Average if it's 60 or 55; Poor if it's 45 or 40; Abysmal if it's below 40 (That doesn't mean you can't start working on changing your rating, one wrong answer at a time.)

SPECIAL NOTE: What do you think about the scoring of 5 points if you answered "yes" for being dissatisfied with your progress (Question 3)? Do you feel that's a mistake that you should add to your Profit IQ for being dissatisfied? It's not a mistake. Keep in mind that progress always starts with dissatisfaction. People who are satisfied vegetate.

THINK LIKE THE OWNER

First, reflect on how you think and feel *now* about the organization that employs you. Then imagine about how your thoughts and actions might change if *you* owned the company or at least a significant piece of it. It's human nature, isn't it, to preserve and protect what is ours? We tend to be a bit careless at times, don't we, with other peoples' property? Start thinking like the owner. If you were in control, how would you respond to customer needs, questions, requests, and complaints? What methods would you think of to make sure forms, supplies, and other assets are not wasted? How could you ensure that workers take care of tools and equipment? How would you deal with problems, hassles, and bottlenecks. How would you improve communication between workers and raise work quality. Once you start thinking like the owner, you start seeing problems—and opportunities—around you.

Teamwork: Your Boss and You

I once asked my boss Phil Brass, when he was executive vice president of Faberge Perfumes Inc., a highly profitable company, how he had made it to the top of a major corporation as a relatively young man.

He thought a moment and then said, "I taught myself to think like the owner."

The profit mindset starts at the top, he explained, and filters down through the ranks. The higher the level of the executive, the more he or she thinks like the owner. "Making money is what business is all about. It stands to reason that the employees the owner—translation, top stockholder—will favor and compensate most generously will be those men and women who contribute most to that bottom line objective."

The higher the level of a manager, the greater the amount of training, experience, and most of all, dedicated effort he or she needs to have in order to deal with the complications that develop in both profit and nonprofit enterprises on a daily basis. When I was employed as systems director at Faberge, I reported directly to Phil. Because he was a top executive, any problem that developed in the office or plant was *his* problem as well as that of the lower level person who worked with the detail. I learned early on to make Phil's problems *my* problems too. It thus stood to reason that any actions or ideas I could come up with that would help ease or eliminate Phil's problems or save him time and effort would make me a favorite in his eyes. The following are a few examples of such instances:

■ A Billing Department Dilemma

The billing workload was heavy—too heavy for the manpower then employed at Faberge and for the office space at hand. The problem was especially noticeable during the busy season, which was from August to Christmas. What to do? My boss's time—taken up with corporate financial responsibilities, labor negotiations, product development problems, and dozens of decisions to ponder—was stretched to the utmost. I viewed the challenge to relieve my boss of the billing workload problem as an important career building opportunity.

As I pondered the problem, the idea of a Working Mother's Swing shift came to me. Mr. Brass loved the concept. We advertised the following day for part-time workers to do billing and invoice-stuffing on a 4:00 PM to Midnight shift. The phone lines were flooded with calls. Home-bound moms with prior clerical experience were delighted by the opportunity to get out of the house for a few hours and earn extra bucks in the process. The operation couldn't have gone more smoothly and efficiently. The billing workload and space problem was soon a thing of the past.

■ Order Tracking

Faberge's cosmetics products were sold on an exclusive basis to selective accounts. The products were very popular. Because mass drug chains were not accepted by Faberge as customers, the chains purchased products from some licensed retailers at a premium. Naturally, this defeated Faberge's purpose.

One day Phil Brass called me to his office and told me he was tearing his hair out in an effort to identify the retailers who made deals with the drug chains. Mr. Rubin, Faberge's owner and major stockholder, was desperate to solve the problem. I said, "Let me think about it." Phil grinned and replied, "Good, then I'll leave it in your hands." "Thanks a lot," I said. It was a tough nut to crack, but I finally did so with a product-coding scheme that identified retailers and gave us a way to call them to task for their actions. Again, a pesky problem was solved.

I relate these stories not to immodestly blow my own horn but to make an important point about the role problem-solving team-work pays in the achievement of career-building goals. Interact with your boss as a problem-solving team and your future will be assured. For the last three or four years of my employment at Faberge, I had intended to resign following bonus time in order to pursue a writing career. Each year, I requested an outrageous pay increase half hoping to be turned down and thus given a reason to leave the company. Each year, however, I got the increase. I attribute those continuing pay boosts to my team-based problem-solving ability that came from my resolution to think like the owner.

> "Interact with your boss as a problem-solving team and your future will be assured."

Despite the pay increases, I finally did quit. But that's another story. All other considerations aside, people are better off doing the kind of work they are best cut out for and most like to do. That just happened to be something different from what I was doing at Faberge. Brilliant as my boss was, he never realized this.

CAN A GOOD IDEA HURT YOU?

In Chapter five, "Learn to be Bold," we discussed the career-busting effects of timidity. In the press, day after day we read stories about outrageous actions corporate CEOs and other top guns take in an effort to beat out competitors. Ironically, however, staff and rank-and-file levels employees who really don't have much to lose often appear to be almost literally afraid of their shadows. Here are a few examples of workers who did and did not take advantage of their good ideas.

■ Frank Murtagh

One day, Frank Murtagh, an ambitious young stockman in an auto parts plant, came up with an idea he thought would cut the time needed to take inventory by a third and cause a reduction in manpower and overtime, thus improving the company's bottom-line performance. Frank was excited. He knew that contributing to profits might not only get him a suggestion award but also would get him in good with his boss and help make him eligible for a wage boost and promotion to Grade I Stockman. He was enthusiastic about his brainstorm, but before he wrote it up he wanted to get a second opinion. So he discussed the idea with Eric who was a long time employee of the department.

Eric gave him a sour look in response. "It's not a bad idea, Frank," his friend said, "but what's wrong with you, are you losing your marbles?"

Frank frowned. "What do you mean?"

"Figure it out for yourself. If your idea works, it'll cut down on overtime and could even throw a couple of guys out of a job. Who do you think is gonna benefit from that?"

Frank didn't like his answer, but what Eric said made sense. He didn't want to be the most unpopular guy in the department.

"Look, pal," Eric said, "are you a company man or one of the guys? Take my advice: Tear up that idea."

Frank took his advice, and is still underpaid and stuck on the shoulder of the career advancement highway. That's not the end of the story. Six months later a suggestion, almost identical to Frank's, was submitted by Gloria, another worker in the department, and it was accepted by management. In addition to receiving a $550 suggestion award, Gloria became a group leader. And instead of being unpopular, she is respected for her brainpower and initiative.

It's a funny thing about good ideas. If you don't cash in on them, someone else will. So who's the smart career climber: Frank or Gloria?

■ Too Good To Submit?

Kim Simpson was in a quandary. As assistant to Mr. Madison, transportation manager at a consumer products company, an important part of her job was to audit freight bills for accuracy. So many errors, accidental or intentional, were made by trucking companies that Kim had learned the companies could not be taken at their word.

One day an advertising mailer from a freight-auditing firm crossed Kim's desk. She had heard about organizations like this. They took over the auditing responsibility in exchange for a portion of the money that would be recovered as a result of inaccurate billing. But she had never given such firms much thought.

The benefits highlighted by the facts and figures in this circular, however, stood out like orange trees in a cornfield. If Mr. Madison hired this firm the auditing job would be done at a fraction of the cost of her salary. But the rub was that her services would no longer be needed. Did it make sense to ease herself out of a job? On the one hand, as an employee it was her responsibility to contribute to her company's profits if she could. On the other hand . . . it was a tough decision to make. She was on the proverbial horns of a dilemma—a dilemma that no one would know about if she kept her mouth shut.

> "It's a funny thing about good ideas. If you don't cash in on them, someone else will."

Because she was worried about what would be the right—and smart—thing to do, Kim took the advertising mailer home to show her dad, a human resources executive at a pharmaceutical company. After reviewing the circular, her father agreed that it would indeed be more profitable for Kim's company to hire this firm. He also conceded that when that was done Kim's services would no longer be needed.

"So wouldn't I be a dummy showing Mr. Madison this mailer?"

"That's a good question," her dad said. "Yes, it could cost you your job. On the other hand, I know that at good companies where employees come up with an idea that would eliminate their own job, the last thing management would do is fire them. Would there be risk involved? It's possible. But I think it's a risk well worth taking."

The next day Kim showed Mr. Madison the mailer and her calculations of how much money the company could save by hiring the freight-auditing firm. Her boss studied the information and enthusiastically agreed with her conclusion.

"Go back to your desk," he instructed Kim.

Her boss left the office and returned a half hour later with a big grin on his face. "The good news is that we're going to hire that auditing firm," he told Kim. "I discussed it with Mr. Evanston. More good news is that his assistant is opting for early retirement and he agrees you would be right for the job."

Kim began working for Mr. Evanston, the company president, and her salary shot up 20 percent.

The point of this story is clear. As Kim's dad told her, any company that fired an employee who came up with an idea resulting in the elimination of his or her own job would be out of its organizational mind. Had that happened in Kim's case, she would have been better off working elsewhere.

IDEAS: BEG, BORROW, OR STEAL 'EM

No consultant, executive, professor, or any other expert on business would deny that—unless your dad owns the company—the number one promoter of increased earnings and career advancement is a well thought-out, profit-building idea.

But as educator and management consultant Leonard J. Smith concedes, "Good ideas aren't easy to find—*unless you keep both eyes and ears open.*"

Smith means this literally. Profit-building ideas are as plentiful as confetti on Times Square at New Year's Eve. So where can you find them? "Anywhere and everywhere," Smith adds. "Right in front of your eyes, inside your organization and out. The smart move is to beg, borrow, or steal them. Ideas are public domain."

■ Jim K.

Eight months ago Jim K., a recent Boston College graduate who ranked in the top third of his class, accepted a job in the marketing department of a machine products corporation. After six months he resigned to accept a job with the company's leading competitor. At his exit interview he gave as his "Reason for Leaving" the explanation that he had never been enrolled in the training program as he had been promised when he was hired.

Jim found his new job much more to his liking. He felt the company was more "people sensitive" and progressive. His training and development program began the first week of his employment. During a training session, the class was briefed on a product development program that had been recently launched. That evening Jim took home a news bulletin describing the program and reread it thoughtfully.

He compared it point by point with a very successful program that was in force at the company he had recently left. After rereading the news bulletin a third time, he showed it to a neighbor who was a marketing executive in a company across town. Then he described the program that was so successful at his ex-employer (his current employer's competitor) and asked what the neighbor thought about the two.

"No question," his neighbor replied. "Your former employer's program has this one beat by a mile."

Jim frowned. "But would it be ethical for me to steal an idea from a former employer?"

His neighbor didn't hesitate. "Are you kidding? Ideas are fair game—unless you tied yourself up by a contract that restricts you from divulging information to a new employer. If you ask me, Jim, this is your chance to make some good brownie points with your new boss."

Jim took his neighbor's advice and persuaded his boss to sit down with him and run a point by point comparison of the two programs. After the session, his boss shook Jim's hand.

"Thanks, Jim, you'll be hearing from me about this."

Keep in mind consultant Leonard Smith's advice: "Ideas are like gold chips wherever they crop up, accidentally or on purpose. Beg, borrow, or steal 'em. It's a wide open market."

■ Kate's Idea

It was a good idea, Ellie agreed. Kate's suggestion to cut procurement costs could save the company a fortune. And it was so simple: Have each department submit a periodic inventory of unused parts, tools, equipment, and supplies. When a department needed something, the supervisor could check the inventory list to see if the company already had the item. Kate had shown her the article in *Industry Week* about the company that had come up with the program and saved a bundle by not ordering supplies it had in stock.

"I checked it out," Kate said. "Department heads and supervisors order dozens of items each year that we already have in stock sitting on shelves or in drawers idle and forgotten. If they only knew that we had the supplies it would eliminate a lot of unneeded procurement. What do you think?"

What did she think? The idea's value was obvious. Kate titled her suggestion form, "Assets Inventory." The reason she told Ellie about it was also obvious. Kate needed her support. Like Kate, Ellie was a key player in the department. And like Kate, she was shooting for an assistant supervisor's job that would be available in a couple of months when Ben Turner retired. If she helped Kate sell a big, money-saving idea to management, it might give her an edge for the job. What to do?

> "Good ideas only hurt you when you don't take advantage of them."

Good question. What would *you* do in Ellie's place?

Ellie asked her husband Bill what he thought she should do. Bill didn't hesitate. "In your shoes I would not only give her your wholehearted support, but I'd also climb right on the bandwagon with her. A good idea can always be made better. I'd give as much thought to Kate's suggestion as you can and tag on some thoughts of your own. Even if Kate is the main contributor, there's no reason you can't share credit with her."

Smart fellow, Bill. Good ideas only you hurt when you don't take advantage of them.

LET'S GET DOWN TO SPECIFICS

Okay, you are convinced, hopefully, that coming up with profit generating ideas is a great asset that will help you open the door to your career growth. Congratulations! Having reached this attitudinal milepost, you have accomplished step one, developing a mindset geared for success. But unless you follow up with step two you will be no better off than you were at the outset. Step two, obviously, is acting on your mindset: You need to ferret out good ideas and put them to work to enhance your company's—and your own—bottom line. But how and from where do you get profit-generating ideas? From three primary sources: the *written word,* the *spoken word,* and the *observant eye.*

> "But how and from where do you get profit-generating ideas? From three primary sources: the *written word,* the *spoken word,* and the *observant eye.*"

The Written Word

Good ideas are yours for the taking. The previous example of Kate's suggestion for an "Assets Inventory" had come to her after she read an article in a magazine slanted to a manufacturing and industrial readership. Hundreds of good ideas appear daily, weekly, and monthly in the nation's newspapers and magazines. That's why people—mostly executives, managers, and supervisors—subscribe to publications. They look to pick up ideas that will help them do their jobs better and more profitably. They read books for the same reason. Isn't that why you are reading *this* book, hoping to pick up ideas to boost your own income and status? If you're short of funds, you don't need to buy or subscribe to publications; you can browse through them in the public library, in your company's reading room, and often on the World Wide Web.

Those with experience know that ideas that boost profits for one company can do the same for other companies as well. An idea that works in one department can work in another department— maybe yours. It makes sense to compile a list of publications that feature articles, tips, pointers, news items, and so forth that deal with processes and procedures pertinent to your own operation or organization. *Where* an idea comes from is of secondary importance. *What the idea can do* for the organization's bottom line is what matters.

Let's examine *Plant Engineering,* a monthly magazine described as a "problem-solving resource for plant engineers," as an example. Every issue of this fact-filled trade journal is loaded with ideas designed to make a plant run easier, faster, more economically, and more profitably. Does your job involve tools or machinery? Do you handle materials and supplies? Are you employed in a plant or warehouse that manufactures products or product components? If so, the odds are high that profit-improvement or cost-reduction ideas in this publication may relate directly or indirectly to your job. If you take the initiative to call a profit-building idea to the attention of management, you could become an overnight hero.

As I thumbed through a recent issue of *Plant Engineering,* I found ideas for:

- ◆ Cutting metal conduit more efficiently.
- ◆ Getting maximum use out of paint rollers.
- ◆ Disposing of messes caused by grease encrustation and buildup.
- ◆ Finding electrical circuit faults.

- Locating gas leaks faster and more effectively.
- Loosening and removing obstinate nuts and bolts from tools and equipment.
- Cleaning the inside of cement and mortar mixers.
- Eliminating eye hazards when grinding metals.

That's just a sampling of available idea-generating material, and this is applicable to only one segment of business. But profit-improvement ideas, small or large, add up. Each one, if cashed in on, will add a notch to your career-boosting belt, and if your company has an award system in place, you should win suggestion awards.

Another example is *Supervision,* a monthly magazine published by the National Research Bureau. It regularly features a column called "Treasure Chest," which is a compilation of "profit improvement and money-saving ideas" applicable to office and plant operations in service and manufacturing operations nationwide. This is in addition to ideas expressed in this useful publication's regular article content.

Scores of other publications and newsletters contain ideas directly or indirectly intended to enhance bottom-line performance. The following is a rundown of examples from the newsletter *Profit Improvement News:* (reprinted with permission)

- An Illinois tool company slashed work glove costs by more than a third. It no longer issues a pair of gloves as a matter of course. Since one glove sustains twice as much wear as the other depending on whether you are right or left-handed, only the worn glove is turned in for replacement.
- Do you sketch units or machines while working on changes, repairs, etc.? This chore consumes precious time. Try snapping a photo instead. Fast, inexpensive, and painless.

◆   Many companies expense computer-programming costs.
     But depending on your earnings and depreciation
     setup, you may benefit by capitalizing this account.
◆   Do you carry a full-time doctor or nurse on the payroll?
     Try contacting your local hospital, advises a manage-
     ment consultant. You may be able to shave medical
     costs by arranging for part-time help.
◆   How much time is killed in your company by employees
     queued up at the office copier—or any other machine?
     This waste can be eliminated by wiring an "IN USE"
     light from the machine to each department from which
     workers come to use the machine. An unlighted bulb
     shows that the unit is available; this is the same system
     used to alert passengers to rest room availability in
     aircraft.

Do any of these ideas sound applicable to your company?
Review enough good ideas and you can be sure some of them will.

The Spoken Word

Abby Daniels, a recent college grad and finance major, was dissatisfied with two aspects of her job in the local bank: (1) her
compensation (2) her job status. A smart lady, she was resolved
to do something about it. People were always telling her how a
major key to career advancement is showing a willingness to help
solve problems that hamper profit performance. She decided to
check this out for herself by working on one particular problem. Periodically, when the bank needed money for investment and
other purposes, it advertised attractive certificate of deposit
rates in the local paper. Following such announcements, a crowd
usually showed up when the bank opened. Often so many people
came that the limited bank staff could not deal with the customers
in a timely manner. Invariably, a percentage of prospective customers became impatient with the long wait and departed.

Abby wondered how this problem could be solved until she discussed it with her friend Susie who worked in another bank across town. "Why don't you suggest doing what we do to solve that problem?" her friend replied. "We set up a table with coffee and doughnuts. Customers are so busy

> "Keeping your eyes open is the simplest and most logical way to pinpoint problems *and* come up with solutions."

snacking and chatting they forget about the time." "Thanks, Susie," Abby said. "Sounds like a great idea."

It was. Don't dismiss simple or obvious solutions—that is what so many good ideas are. The number of departing customers dropped dramatically after the bank set up a refreshment table, and Abby's value rose to new heights in the eyes of management.

Word of mouth is a great way to get good ideas. You can take advantage of this "profit directed communication vehicle" in two ways: (1) by keeping your ears open when problems are aired and discussed and (2) by asking around—friends, neighbors, relatives, coworkers, etc.—when a problem that needs a solution comes to your attention.

The Observant Eye

Keeping your eyes open is the simplest and most logical way to pinpoint problems *and* come up with solutions. "I have never seen an organization of any kind," says marketing expert and publishing guru Richard R. Conarroe, "that is not beset with problems on a day-to-day basis. Often problems are so obvious, you trip over them. Yet employees see right through them without really looking."

Do you want to gain a reputation in your company as an ace problem solver? Richard Conarroe offers the following advice: "Sit

"When customers don't profit, neither does the supplier, and neither do you."

down with a pencil and a sheet of paper and call to mind as many projects, processes, or situations as you can that are plagued by bottlenecks or hassles or are cost-inefficient. Then rally your own experience, along with the input of respected friends and associates, and add a dash of creative thought to the problem at hand. You may be surprised by what you come up with."

As Richard Conarroe notes, more often than not, the problems are right there in front of you. You may be so accustomed to living with them that you give them no thought. All you have to do is zero in and start focusing.

RECRUIT THE CUSTOMER TO YOUR TEAM

If problems are opportunities, dissatisfied customers are the freight trains that make them stop at your station. Unhappy customers cause a company to lose profits faster than an open fire hydrant loses water. Obviously, the key to sustained profit performance is making sure customers receive **trouble-free business interactions frequently.**

"Too often," says Robert E. Levinson, Marketing Vice President at Lynn University, "employees take customer service for granted."

As this expert suggests, every supervisor and executive should hang the following sign in front of his or her desk:

"The customer is doing you a favor when he calls, not the other way around."

Whatever your level in the hierarchy, you, too, would do well to post this sign in a conspicuous place, if your goals are to win promotion, impress the influentials who count in your company, and multiply your earnings. Identify causes of customer dissatisfaction and help eliminate them. Always ask customers if they have had any problems interacting with your company. Dream up imaginative, new ways to make your company's products or services more profitable for the customer. Most importantly, every personal sacrifice you make to boost customer satisfaction will be an important milestone—noted by those who count—on your trip to the executive suite.

CHAPTER LESSONS

✓ Problems = Opportunities. Come up with a fix for a problem that is reducing your employer's bottom line, and you will get noticed and move up.

✓ There are three types of job performers: the **Simple Negatives**, the **Simple Positives**, and the **Special Elites.** Simple Negatives are workers who barely get by, whose work performance is substandard. Simple Positives are those who are hardworking, dependable, and valued by their bosses, but they are not innovators or volunteers. They will enjoy only slow, but steady career growth. Special Elites are the innovators, volunteers, and idea generators of the workplace. They are America's future top executives and leaders—everyone should aspire to be a "Special Elite."

✓ Think like the owner. Treat the company as if it were your own and you will start seeing problems—or opportunities—everywhere.

✓ Work with your boss to solve problems that increase the department's or company's bottom line, and he or she won't forget it.

✓ Cash in on your good ideas—or someone else will.

✓ The ability to generate profit-building ideas is an excellent skill to have and will open the door to career growth.

✓ Use the resources around you to come up with profit-generating ideas. These ideas come from the **written word**, the **spoken word**, and the **observant eye.**

✓ Read newspapers, magazines, books, and surf the World Wide Web to help you generate ideas for raising your employer's bottom line.

✓ The customer is doing you a favor when he or she calls with a problem or complaint—not the other way around. Put the customer first and find a way to fix the problem. You will end up both keeping the customer for the company and raising the company's bottom line.

Chapter 10:
Welcome Change

Problem: You're Fearful of Change
Rx: Change the Status Quo to Status Go

"He that will not apply new remedies must expect new evils."
—Francis Bacon, Author and Philosopher

Do you sometimes feel perplexed by or even nervous about the prospect of change? If so, welcome to the club. Read what some of history's so-called "voices of authority" had to say on the subject as quoted by *Newsweek:*

"Airplanes are interesting toys but of no military value."
—Marshal Ferdinand Foch, World War I Commander, 1911

"Who the hell wants to hear actors talk?"
—Harry M. Warner, Warner Brothers, 1927

"There is no reason for an individual to have a computer in their home."
—Kenneth Olsen, President/Founder, Digital Equipment Corporation, 1977

"Computers in the future may . . . perhaps only weigh 1.5 tons."
—*Popular Mechanics,* 1949

"Man will never reach the moon."
—Dr. Lee DeForest, Father of Radio, 1967

"Everything that can be invented has been invented"
—Charles H. Duell, U.S. Commissioner of Patents, 1899

"For the majority of people, the use of tobacco has a beneficial effect."
—Dr. Ian G. MacDonald, Surgeon, 1963

Sometimes you don't know whom to believe when change is headed your way. But for the time being we'll stick with famed industrialist Charles Kettering who said: "The world hates change, yet it is the only thing that has brought progress."

If your career goal is to increase both your income and status, we'd suggest that, from a career standpoint at least, you hop aboard and think of change as bringing progress.

Within the past decade or two we have seen more technological change than in all of previously recorded history. But changes have not been confined only to technology. The face of marketing and merchandising has altered dramatically—the way customers are served, the way people access and evaluate information, the way employees are hired and evaluated, and the way stocks are traded. But most importantly are the changes in the way careers are launched and the way staffers who are amenable to change turn into high-level executives, sometimes overnight.

> "A willingness to change is a primary ingredient of success."

A willingness to change is a primary ingredient of success. So far as your career is concerned, you have three options open to you:

1. **You can resist change.** *As history shows us, resisters fall behind.*
2. **You can go along with change.** *Those who go along with change get along and grow gradually.*
3. **You can *initiate* change.** *The initiators are those imaginative men and women who climb the career ladder three or four rungs at a time.*

Where do you fit into the picture? Take the following quiz to find out. The more honestly and objectively you respond to the questions below, the more accurate your self-evaluation will be.

(Note: If you do not own this copy of Job Smarts, then be sure to make a photocopy of this quiz before you mark your answers.)

	YES	NO
1. When change is proposed, is your initial reaction to stick with the system with which you're familiar?	___	___
2. When someone suggests an idea do you often promise to give it some thought, then, intentionally or not, forget about it?	___	___
3. Are you usually receptive to ideas that are presented by lower ranking employees?	___	___
4. Do you generally allow time to digest a new idea before venturing an opinion?	___	___
5. Do you stay alert to your company's problems and roadblocks in an effort to come up with solutions and improvements?	___	___
6. In evaluating a proposed change, do you usually consider the long-range as well as the short-range effects?	___	___
7. Do you believe that change is sometimes useful for the sake of change alone?	___	___
8. Do you usually keep the company's bottom line in mind when suggesting or evaluating a change?	___	___
9. Do you make it your business to keep abreast of the latest developments in your field?	___	___
10. Did you submit three or more suggestions to your supervisor within the past six months?	___	___
11. Do you allow yourself a sufficient cushion of time to devote to creative thinking?	___	___

	YES	NO

12. Do you sometimes brusquely oppose suggested change because you fear it will saddle you with more work?   ___   ___

13. Do you always make sure you thoroughly understand a proposed change before either endorsing or rejecting it?   ___   ___

14. When you have a change to propose, do you appreciate the importance of recruiting allies to support your idea?   ___   ___

15. If someone submits an idea you feel is useless do you ever ridicule him or her?   ___   ___

16. When an idea is presented do you automatically oppose it if you feel it won't benefit you even though it will benefit the company?   ___   ___

17. When an idea is proposed, do you allow your personal prejudice against the proponent to influence your judgment?   ___   ___

18. When a good idea is presented do you usually try to hop on the bandwagon and contribute ideas of your own in support?   ___   ___

19. In presenting or considering an idea are you usually sensitive to the human factors involved?   ___   ___

20. If you weren't keen on an idea presented by a buddy of yours, would you support it anyway?   ___   ___

21. When you come up with a proposed change do you usually consult the people who will be affected by it?   ___   ___

22. If your boss proposes an idea you don't like, do you level with him or her and offer your honest opinion?   ___   ___

23. Do you understand the importance of good timing in presenting an idea to your boss?   ___   ___

	YES	NO

24. If an idea is hard to sell, do you solicit the aid of an influential supervisor or executive? ___ ___

25. Do you (or would you) encourage subordinates to submit ideas to you? ___ ___

Calculate your receptivity to change.

On some of the above questions the "yea's" have it; on others the "nay's" have it. Tally your score and see how you rate as a proponent and supporter of constructive change. Give yourself one point each if you answered "no" to Questions 1, 2, 12, 15, 16, 17, and 20. Give yourself one point for each of the other questions to which you entered "yes." Now add the total number of points and enter your score below.

Your Score ___

How do you rate?

If your score is 21 or higher—congratulations. You rate well as an innovator and initiator of change; 18 to 20 is better than average; 15 to 17 mediocre to fair. If your score is 14 or lower, you have your work cut out for you. Start disciplining yourself to think of constructive change as a friend and opportunity booster instead of a hardship and inconvenience.

WHAT ARE YOU AFRAID OF?

History proves repeatedly that change—intelligently proposed, communicated, and initiated—is most often beneficial, not only to organizations, but also to the individuals employed there, *including those who opposed it.* In survey after survey conducted in companies where major change affecting workers has occurred, more than 90 percent of employees have responded "yes" to the question, *Are you better off now than before the new system?*

Why then do so many people resist change? Psychologists cite as a general explanation, "fear of the unknown." But when we get down to specifics, we see a variety of reasons emerge. Here are some of the most commonly cited causes for resistance to change. How many can you identify with because they ring true to your personal experience?

"It will create more work for me."

In some cases change does result in more work for individual employees. In other situations this concern turns out to be unjustified. Constructive change usually reduces the workload of employees. But think about this. From your point of view, if a change does result in more work for you, is this necessarily detrimental to your career? Is your current workload unreasonably burdensome, or could you reasonably take on some new responsibilities? From a career advancement standpoint, the more *productive* you are, the more *valuable* you are to your employer. As many employers can tell you, those who voluntarily take on added responsibilities have taken a large step on the path to job advancement and growth.

■ Good Change: George

George was a recent high school graduate, and he worked for a New Jersey toy company operating a billing machine. He was dissatisfied with his job because he saw little if any chance for advancement. One day he was informed that a new billing system, which used sophisticated equipment, was scheduled to be installed. This was the final straw, George thought. Not only was he unhappy at his job, but now he also had to learn to use the new equipment. He figured the new system would probably increase his workload and add further stress to his workday. George was on the verge of

> "Approach change not as a hardship and inconvenience but as a challenge to prove your value as a team player."

quitting when his boss advised him to hang in there. "You won't be sorry," he promised. George wasn't. He became skilled at operating the new equipment and thus increased his value to the company. When performance evaluation time rolled around a month later, George got a nice raise and his job classification was upgraded.

"The new system (or procedure) is too complicated."

This can be a valid concern. Most often, we feel that what is new is more complicated and less comfortable than what we were familiar with and understood. However, the feelings only last *until the new system becomes second nature to us as we use it repeatedly, after which it almost invariably becomes simpler and more efficient.* The reason a system is changed in the first place is to fix old glitches, make jobs more efficient, and improve operations overall. If the systems experts do their jobs, a new operation should be more pleasant and user-friendly. The idea is to approach change not as a hardship and inconvenience but as a challenge to prove your value as a team player. When a change is proposed or initiated, the new system isn't the only thing that's on trial. Employees are also "on trial" as management watches their responses—positive or negative—and evaluates who has the company's interests in mind.

■ **Good Change: Susan**

When the new reporting procedure was explained, Susan thought she would never understand it. She felt it would take months or even a year to grasp the process. But a month or so after the procedure was in place and operating, Susan was amazed to find that she felt like she had been working with it for years. She even remarked to her supervisor, "I don't know why somebody didn't come up with this idea a long time ago. It's so much simpler and takes so much less time." As Susan learned, the anxiety you feel about becoming familiar with something new is almost always more formidable than the new process itself.

"The proposed change will undermine my job and status."

If you have this feeling, the problem may be that the innovation wasn't adequately communicated and its job-related effects clearly explained to you. Ideally, your first move when a change is proposed is to make it your business to understand what the expected consequences will be. Decades ago when computers took over manual processing in thousands of organizations, poor communication was cited as the main reason for problems arising—many employees quit to find other jobs because they feared being fired. If you're afraid an impending change will adversely affect your job, clear the air by confiding whatever apprehensions you might have to your supervisor. You may find your fears are needless.

■ **Good Change: Jerry**

The rumors were spreading faster than wildfire in a drought. Automated equipment had been ordered to handle a large assembly operation in the plant. Consultants had been hired to evaluate the operation and were in constant conference with the plant manager and supervisors. Jerry, a key staffer in the semi-manual operation, figured the rumors were probably true. It looked like a shake-up was in the making. A handful of employees were checking the newspaper's classified ads every night for job openings; three had already resigned and moved on. Jerry had advanced nicely during his two years on the job. He liked the company, and he liked the way he was treated. It didn't make sense, he thought, to quit without making an effort to determine how his prospects would be affected by the coming change.

Jerry confided his concerns to his boss who frowned in response. "It's pretty obvious, isn't it? You're right, new equipment has been ordered and a restructuring has been planned. Management should have announced and defined the plan weeks ago. But I can tell you this. For one thing, you will be trained to operate the new equipment. For another, the equipment itself is a secondary factor in determining an operation's success; far more important are experienced workers with a depth of knowledge about departmental needs and goals. By the time you are trained and the new system is in full operation, you will be more valuable to the company than you ever were, and my guess is that you will be compensated accordingly."

"The change was imposed instead of proposed."

A change imposed is almost certain to be opposed. For innovation to work smoothly and efficiently, the full cooperation of the individuals—from supervisors to entry-level employees—responsible for doing the job is essential. Failure to consult everyone in advance is a major cause of resistance. This is a key point to remember when you evaluate a change proposed by others or consider a change you hope to initiate yourself.

■ Bad Change: Anita

Flextime had been an option half-heartedly offered by the company for the past three years or so. This was a big plus for Anita, who had an eight-year-old son she had to drive to and pick up from school. One day she was informed by her supervisor that flextime was being eliminated and rigid work hours would apply to all employees. Anita was shocked and wanted to know why. Her supervisor shrugged. "Flextime didn't work out." Anita, along with several other employees, resigned. By the time management realized that imposing change without consulting the people affected rarely—if ever—works out, several key employees were gone.

"I don't think the change is necessary."

If you don't see the need for a proposed change, the fault may be management's, not yours. When a new system affecting employees' work lives is proposed, the proponent owes it to the people who will work with the new setup to explain why the change is needed, how it will contribute to the bottom line, and how it is expected to improve the system that is being replaced. It's your supervisor's responsibility to get this message across. When you are the initiator it is *your* responsibility to clarify the benefits involved and the profit improvement anticipated. Clearly communicating these aspects of change is an absolute must if you hope to sell your idea successfully.

■ Good Change: Mary

Mary had played an important role in the Payroll Department of a stationery products distributor for almost six years and enjoyed good seniority. When the news was announced that Payroll was going to be absorbed by the General Office, she couldn't see the reason for it. On top of that she was afraid it might adversely affect her status and seniority. There might even be a reduction in personnel, which was often the case when a restructuring was made. Her friend Peggy advised, "You'd better start looking around so you won't be left high and dry when the ax falls." Instead of taking Peggy's advice, Mary talked to her supervisor. "Mr. Adams," she asked, "why is this change necessary and how will it affect my job?" "Good questions, Mary," he replied. "Making Payroll part of General Office will make photocopies and other equipment more accessible to both operations. It will result in the saving of some much needed space. And it will make more computers available for people to work on. A projected profit improvement in excess of $50,000 a year is anticipated. How will it affect your job? Not at all, so far as I can see, except that you will be a little less crowded."

Moral of the story: It always pays to investigate before jumping to conclusions.

"It will be too hard for me to master the new setup; I'll be fired."

If you feel mastering the new system will be difficult, readjust your thinking to view this challenge as a plus instead of a minus. This holds particularly true where new technology is involved. Countless cases could be cited where employees, after acquiring new skills and learning the new system, advanced a level or more in the corporate hierarchy and were compensated accordingly. The tougher the new system is to master, the greater is your opportunity for advancement.

■ **Arthur's Lesson**

An Applications Software Provider (ASP) was being installed in the plant, and Arthur, a service equipment mechanic, was afraid it would be too difficult for him to understand. If he failed to master working with the equipment, he figured he'd end up being fired. So he might as well quit now while the job market was hot. Arthur resigned his good job and started shopping the job market. The first two managers that interviewed him asked the same question: "Are you familiar with ASP?" Of course, he wasn't. Eventually Arthur landed a job. But what a waste! Had he stuck with his old job instead of quitting so hastily, he already would have had the ASP training he needed and would be well ahead of the game.

"The new system will reduce my overtime."

That may very well be true. In fact, excessive overtime might be a large reason for the change in the first place. So it's up to you to decide whether your economic future is more dependent on working long hours or on acquiring more knowledge. Example after example shows that when major systems innovations are made, employees who are most successful in mastering the new operation and working with it effectively are the ones who climb the career ladder faster and higher.

■ **Good Change: Cal**

Cal worked as a stock handler in a beverage distributing plant. He had gotten word through the grapevine that a new system being installed would result in overtime hours being substantially cut. Cal considered himself underpaid now; the new setup would reduce his wages even more. "Why don't you talk it over with dad?" his wife Emily suggested. "Get his advice." Cal's father was a seasoned plant executive. "If I were in your shoes," his dad said, "I would view this as an opportunity. Instead of putting in those long hours, I would register for some evening courses and get your high school diploma. That way you will boost your chances for a better job where you won't have to depend on overtime to earn a decent wage." With a bit of a prod from Emily, Cal followed his dad's advice. Now, for the first time in his career, he is starting to climb the corporate ladder instead of spinning his wheels.

"Most of my coworkers oppose the change. I'd be an outcast if I went along with it."

The question for you to answer is this: Would you rather be popular or prosperous? One reality of life in the marketplace is that most people aren't ambitious. They prefer "pleasant" work conditions to working their butts off to get ahead. But, as you must realize, growth without hard work is unlikely unless your dad owns the company. If career growth is your goal, your coworkers' lack of ambition can work in your favor. It cuts down on the competition for those tougher and better paying jobs. Hard work is one of the keys to getting to the top. It's no coincidence that the highest ranking and highest paid executives are the ones who work hardest to learn more and contribute more to the company's bottom line.

■ Good Change: Phyllis

According to Phyllis's calculations, her idea for processing mail faster and more efficiently would save the company an estimated $4,000 to $6,000 a month. She was enthusiastic about her brainstorm, had visions of receiving a nice suggestion award, and thought a promotion might come along as well. But other members of the Mail Department were dead set against the proposal. Some were so angry they wouldn't even talk to her. "You'd better smarten up," Lucy advised, "if you don't want to be an outcast around here." Phyllis replied, "If helping to benefit the operation and improve my career makes me an outcast. I guess I've found the right direction to go." Smart woman.

"This change means I will no longer work with my close friends and associates."

Big deal. So you'll make new close friends and associates, gain new skills, and may earn more in the process. Disrupting social relationships may seem unpleasant. But nothing is more unpleasant than spinning your wheels. Two of the surest ways to avoid career blockage are to cooperate with innovation and to initiate change.

■ Good Change: Alice

Employees lined up on both sides of the fence when the new incentive system was installed in Accounts Payable. Those on one side of the fence were helpful and cooperative; those on the other used every excuse they could find to resist the change. Alice was one of the most helpful employees. She was not only cooperative, but she also suggested ideas to make the system work even more successfully than management had anticipated. Her positive approach was recognized and appreciated. Before long she was promoted out of the Accounts Payable department to a more important job in Accounting. She missed working side by side with old friends and going to lunch with them. But Alice quickly made new friends in Accounting. Some of them were at a higher hierarchical level than her buddies in Accounts Payable, which, from a career advancement perspective, wasn't bad at all.

"I'm worried about my job security."

This is an invalid concern 99 percent of the time. In today's marketplace in particular, the greatest job security is enjoyed by those men and women who can list numerous skills and experiences on their resumes. Every new systems or operational change offers a learning opportunity and the chance to add another notch to your career belt.

■ Apply simple logic

Question: If you were able to scrutinize the resumes of 100 top industry leaders, what do you think they would all have in common? Answer: Every one would feature an impressively long rundown of management and/or technological skills and experience. Do you think these highly paid executives are worried about job security?

> "The greatest job security is enjoyed by those men and women who can cite the most skills and experience on their resumes."

WHEN THE INNOVATOR IS THE OTHER GUY

Business is competition—between corporations and between people. General Motors, for example, is in competition with Toyota and DaimlerChrysler for customers. You're in competition with Frank, Harry, and Jane for that better job, that prestigious assignment.

So what is the best course of action to take when your coworker Lucille wants a promotion as badly as you do, comes up with a great idea that will unquestionably raise her a notch or two in management's estimation? Should you support the suggested change? Resist it? Or just sit there like a lump?

Don't be a "lump." You have to take some kind of constructive action. If the idea really is good, join in and try to add your improvements.

■ Charley's Dilemma

When Barry came up with the idea to combine purchase orders and requisitions into a single form his office manager was enthusiastic. Machine operators and other staff people in Purchasing agreed that it would simplify the operation and save the company money. The controller was all for the change. Everybody seemed in favor of it—everybody, that is, but Charley, who, like Barry, was one of the department's key players.

Not that he didn't *appreciate* Barry's brainstorm. Charley had to concede it was brilliant, and the report Barry had turned in to sell the concept to management was a great piece of work. Charley's problem was that he and Barry were in competition for a promotion to group leader. This suggestion, when accepted, could put Barry well ahead in the race.

So Charley gave the matter some serious thought. On the one hand, Barry needed his support. As a key employee in the department, his opposition could delay the change. On the other hand, Charley reasoned, the idea had definite merit and would be accepted whether he resisted it or not. Also, it was his responsibility as a loyal employee to work for profit improvement. Wouldn't he be better off showing himself to be a supporter rather than a spoiler? Darned right, he would!

Charley wisely chose to be a supporter. On top of that, he decided to go a step further. He prepared and submitted his own well thought out report, not only supporting Barry's idea, but at the same time contributing a proposal of his own to strengthen the idea even more. Charley included convincing figures to prove that it would be profitable as well to set up a "Notebook Memo Procedure" that would eliminate the need to prepare a purchase order and requisition form for orders amounting to $50 or less. This would save supervisors valuable time and effort, not to mention create less paperwork.

Barry liked Charley's idea, appreciated his support, and added Charley's report as a supplement to his own. When management wholeheartedly accepted the suggestion, Charley wound up sharing in the glory instead of being dubbed a resister, which would have hurt his team-player image.

■ Denise's Brainstorm

Customers come and go. When they go faster than they come, it spells trouble. Customer Service Representative Denise, a recent college grad, saw the writing on the wall. Her company was in trouble because of its outdated customer service program. Thanks in part to an idea Denise got from a lecture by her marketing professor that she had recorded, Denise came up with a brainstorm for revising the program. When she dug out the tape and adapted the concept to the company's needs, she was confident that it would succeed in enticing customers instead of turning them off.

The problem was that the system her program would replace had been conceived and installed by her boss. Denise's proposal would imply that her boss's system was flawed. Unless . . .

Denise was no dummy. Instead of presenting her idea as an innovation, she suggested it as a program *improvement*. This made a world of difference from her boss's perspective. His image would be enhanced rather than tarnished by Denise's proposal. Her strategy worked. So did the program—not only to the company's advantage, but also to Denise's.

In sharing the credit with a key company player—*her boss, no less*—Denise's personal image and reputation received a career-boosting jolt. She also got a fat increase in her take-home pay.

"BUT IF I CHANGE MY JOB I'LL LOSE MY BENEFITS"

This consideration depends on your situation, of course. But losing your benefits could be one of the most *beneficial* moves you'll ever make. A major corporate goal in today's changing marketplace is to hang on to qualified and experienced employees. An Ohio manufacturing company is notorious for "paying in the dark" as the expression goes. But it makes up for its below-average compensation structure with a seemingly attractive pension program that gives workers who remain employed for many years a big bundle of cash when they retire. "The pension," according to one consultant, "is nothing more than a sour plum dangling from a far-off tree. Many employees would be much better off," he adds, "forgoing the pension, and shopping for greener pastures where the compensation would be greater as would the opportunity for advancement."

The consultant cites one case in which a talented engineer employed by a chintzy company decides to make extra money selling his ideas to a competitor. He is too insecure to quit his inadequately compensated job, but he feels cheated by his company and justified in cheating his employer in return. You reap what you sow, he rationalizes. The engineer is frustrated and bitter, an undesirable way to spend a career.

Stuck in a Rut?

These days there's no reason to be stuck in a bad job, especially if you are young and healthy. Nonetheless some people hang on, and for more reasons than because they succumb to the bait of a seemingly attractive pension plan. Many endure corporate abuse and unfair treatment by a hated boss because they're afraid to quit for fear of losing their insurance coverage. If you find yourself in this boat, read on.

> "There's no reason to be stuck in a bad job, especially if you are young and healthy."

The 1996 Health Insurance Portability and Accountability Act (HIPAA) ensures that anyone with health insurance can get coverage from private companies in the state they work in even if they lose their job or switch jobs. That's true. But as *Newsweek* writer Ellen Spragins points out, "there's no guarantee you will be able to afford it." In several states HIPAA policies can cost up to six times the price of a standard policy. "Searching for the best price is crucial," Spragins writes. Her advice: Apply to as many carriers as possible. When the policies arrive, compare prices, and pick the one that looks best.

A well-reputed financial advisor's assistance can't hurt. "With good planning," says Spragins, "HIPAA can still help unblock job lock."

STICK OR QUIT?

Hypothesis: You are a young, ambitious, educated (preferably college degreed, or enrolled in a program to upgrade your education) worker, and you feel you are underpaid after you have compared salaries for similar jobs in the area. If this roughly defines your situation, there are only two actions to take to avoid becoming a career chicken:

◆ Launch an in-house effort to bring your earnings and opportunities up to par.

◆ While still employed, float feeder lines in the marketplace to see how much better you can do. Keep in mind, of course, that your actual earnings figure—the dollar amount—is not the only measure of a desirable job. Advancement potential and the opportunity to learn are equally important factors contributing to job satisfaction. Also, you may need to relocate to improve your career chances.

What Grabs You Most?

Step one in your "Personal Career Advancement Program" is an evaluation of your skills, experience, interests, and values— all reviewed objectively. Consider the following factors and give yourself a 1 through 10 priority rating for each of the statements (10 is the lowest priority, 1 the highest).

Priority Rating

Friendship and sociability in the workplace	_____
Family and friends in your current location	_____
Status in the corporate hierarchy	_____
Opportunity to increase knowledge	_____
Leadership opportunity	_____
A chance to upgrade your job skills	_____
Respect and admiration for your company and its leaders	_____
Ease of work commute	_____
Benefits package—insurance, vacation, holidays, and so forth	_____
Freedom to work without supervision	_____
Job interest—your job fits you like a glove	_____

Career evaluation is a highly personalized procedure. Relate each of the ratings on page 226 to the job you currently hold, paying special attention to those items you ranked 1 through 3. If your job fails to satisfy many of your 1 through 3 priorities, you may be ready to explore greener pastures.

Ready and Waiting

Keep in mind that there is never a better time than now to begin your Personal Career Advancement Program so you can land your 1 through 3 rated dream job. If your job at your present company is unsatisfactory, it might be time for you to check out the competition and find a position that fulfills your 1 through 3 priorities. Why settle for a merely *good* job at a *good* company when you, thanks to technology, have access to the *best?*

The place to check out America's best and most popular employers is on the World Wide Web. Web sites filled with company information are available to everyone at the click of a mouse. If you don't own a computer, you can surf the Web at your local library. One site to check out, for example, is http://www.fortune.com, which has the list "100 Best Companies To Work For." These "best companies" include Synovus Financial Corporation, SAS Institute, Deloitte & Touche, MBNA, and Hewlett-Packard.

WomensWire.com (www.womenswire.com/work/work3.html) features the list "Best Employers for Women," which you can view alphabetically or by location. Included are such favorites as Home Box Office and NationsBank in Atlanta; Amoco Corporation and Northern Trust in Chicago; Brogan & Partners and Compuware Corporation in Detroit; Patagonia in Los Angeles; and Hanna Andersson in Portland.

The *best of the bunch* are out there and waiting for you. With a click of the mouse you can start down your career path to advancement. Go get 'em, and the best of luck!

CHAPTER LESSONS

✓ Accept change as a positive factor in your personal and career growth.

✓ Look before you leap. When change at your workplace is imminent, don't act without thinking. Ask your boss how the planned change will affect your job. Keep a positive attitude about change; your boss won't forget it.

✓ Be a team player. Support your coworkers' good ideas for change; it might help you get noticed, too.

✓ Learn to assess what's important in your life and use these factors as a gauge to help you to decide to stay at a job or move on to pastures that would be greener for you.

INDEX